THE PSYCHOLOGY OF
THE WITCHER

T0244531

THE PSYCHOLOGY OF
THE WITCHER

EDITED BY ANTHONY M. BEAN, PHD

Leyline Publishing, Inc.
Fort Worth, TX

Book © 2024 by Anthony M. Bean

Introduction © 2024 by Cody Pondsmith

"The Law Of Surprise: Willfulness and Surender In The Story Of Geralt of Rivia" © 2024 by Brian Adams

"Geralt As A Masculine Construct: When The Only Things That Are Toxic Are The Potions" © 2024 by Melissa Huntley and Cassandra Buck

"Brotherhood Knows No Bounds, Only Bonds" © 2024 by Abbigail Pollack

"Wait-Who Are We Supposed To Be Fighting? Rehumanization In The Witcher" © 2024 by Alex Baker

"They are People: The Witcher And The Wounded Healer" © 2024 by Bryan C. Duncan

"The White Wolf's Gray Hair: Ethics Are Not Black And White" © 2024 by Lou Anna Claveau

"Searching For Connection: Types of Love In The Witcher" © 2024 by Wendi "Nicki" Line

"Four Phases of Yennefer: Self-Determination Theory And Yennefer's Personal Development" © 2024 by Joe Leconte

 "Yennefer's Fight For Freedom In The Witcher Universe: Exploring Her Path Through The Lens of Liberation Psychologies" © 2024 by Sylwia Korsak

"Sexual And Relationship Orientations In The Witcher" © 2024 by Wendi "Nicki" Line

"How To Toss A Coin To The Witcher: Reward And Purpose While Impacting The World" © 2024 by Daniel A. Kaufmann

Leyline Publishing, Inc.
7801 Oakmont Blvd, Suite 101
Fort Worth, Texas 76132
leylinepublishing.com | geektherapeutics.com

Printed in the United States of America
10 9 8 7 6 5 4 3 2 1

Library of Congress Cataloging-in-Publication Data is available upon request.

978-1-955406-26-0 (trade paper)
978-1-955406-41-3 (e-book)
978-1-955406-42-0 (Audio Book)

Editing by Anthony M. Bean
Copyediting and Proofreading by Kate Hollis
Text Design and composition by Asya Blue
Cover Design and Illustration by Arianna "Kaz" Unciano

DEDICATION

To Andrzej Sapkowski, whose brilliant mind gave birth to a world where monsters and men are equally fascinating.

To the creators at CD Projekt Red, for bringing that world to life with unparalleled passion and artistry.

To the fans of The Witcher, who find solace and strength in the tales of Geralt, Yennefer, and Ciri.

And to those who, like Geralt, are always searching—may you find what you seek, and may your path be guided by your own inner compass.

CONTENTS

INTRODUCTION

"People . . . like to invent monsters and monstrosities.
Then they seem less monstrous themselves. When they
get blind-drunk, cheat, steal, beat their wives, starve an
old woman, when they kill a trapped fox with an axe or
riddle the last existing unicorn with arrows, they like
to think that the Bane entering cottages at daybreak is
more monstrous than they are. They feel better then.
They find it easier to live."

— Geralt of Rivia

These words lie at the heart of the vastly popular Polish fantasy franchise, *The Witcher*. In this world, very real monsters roam the forests and swamps of the Continent, stealing away children, eating farmhands, and placing curses on unsuspecting villagers. But the beasts that lurk in the darkness are rarely presented as the primary villains. No, in the world of *The Witcher*, the most dangerous monster is human nature. Pride, greed, lust, hatred, and envy are powerful forces which can drive people to do terrible things. Nowhere is this better illustrated than through the witchers themselves.

The main character of the *Witcher* saga is Geralt of Rivia, one of a number of superhuman warriors called witchers, who travel the Continent, killing monsters, to protect villagers and nobles alike. In any other setting, Geralt and his kin would be valiant heroes, beloved by the peasants and respected by the nobility. But this is far from the case. Witchers are reviled by the people and

1

THE PSYCHOLOGY OF THE WITCHER

only ever tolerated for their skill at monster-slaying. When Geralt enters a village, the women and children flee indoors, and the men clutch their pitchforks. To them, the "witch men" are mutants who feel nothing but cold greed and burning lust. Any dealing with a witch man could end in your death . . . or worse. Unsurprisingly, this false narrative goes all the way back to the creation of witchers.

Decades ago, the mages of the North came together to find a solution to the epidemic of monsters. Their answer was to create valiant monster-slaying knights to protect all of humanity from the monstrosities of the wilderness. Of course, this was only the public reason. The project was funded by the monarchs of the North, who were less interested in freeing their people from the dangers of monsters and more interested in creating super soldiers to fight their wars for them. With these goals in sight, the most powerful sorcerers and sorceresses came together to turn regular humans into magic-wielding knights with supernatural speed, heightened senses, and indomitable resilience.

But they failed.

Time and time again, the mages failed to create their ideal warriors. Each failure resulted in the agonizing death of their subject. As the years wore on, the mages turned to mutating children, whose bodies were more capable of handling the mutation process. Hundreds of children were taken off the street or purchased from their impoverished parents to be fodder for this experiment. And they all died in agony at the hands of the mages.

In the end, the best that could be created were the witchers, named for their minor control of magic which was labeled "witchery" by the mages. When the monarchs lost their trust in the mages and funding dried up, the witchers were abandoned by all but a few of the mages. They had been tortured, mutated, and dehumanized, and they knew that now their only purpose in life was to kill. They began to travel the realms, slaying monsters, but the people of the Continent could only see them as mutants and freaks. Despite driving so many species of monsters to extinction and saving so many lives, the witchers were ostracized by society. Eventually, this all-consuming hatred and fear would boil over, and the people turned on the witchers. One by one, the witcher's keeps fell as humans, who were pushed to violence by their hatred of the witchers or their envy of the witchers' knowledge, laid siege to them.

By the time the first stories of the saga begin, witchers are a bygone species, numbering no more than ten or twenty at most. Through the eyes of Geralt of Rivia, we see how the world has fared after the witchers' near extinction. In the absence of monsters, there's nothing to distract from the monstrous behavior of humanity. Kings wage war simply to gain new territory, throwing conscripts into the front lines to be torn to pieces. Mages scheme and plot, playing dangerous games of politics that ruin countless lives. Brutal, amoral people rise to the top of society to rule over their subjects with an iron fist. Even when the monsters begin to return, through the eyes of a witcher we see how these dangers are brought about by human error. Thoughtless decisions made out of lust, envy, and greed give birth to terrible curses. Cold-blooded murder attracts corpse-eating beasts from the woods. In many of the stories in the *Witcher* saga and video games, there is a terrible action or inaction at the heart of the problem which brought the monster's reign of terror about.

This human-focused take on classical fantasy is one of the reasons *The Witcher* resonates with so many people. Monsters are a nebulous concept, something we can't truly relate to. But human greed, human error, violent selfishness—these all hit home. The stories in *The Witcher* are stories about people that happen to have monsters in them, and this makes them special.

But this is only one take on the psychology of *The Witcher*. This rich franchise is filled with different ideologies held by conflicting characters and mindsets that take a great deal of contextualization to make sense of. This book sets out to unravel all of these psychological aspects to better understand the fascinating world of *The Witcher*.

—Cody Pondsmith, Creator of *The Witcher TRPG*

1

THE LAW OF SURPRISE: WILLFULNESS AND SURRENDER IN THE STORY OF GERALT OF RIVIA

BRIAN ADAMS

*"Well, we're afeared. And what of it? Do we sit
down and weep and tremble? Life must go on.
And what will be, will be. What is destined can't be
avoided, in any case."*

– Geralt of Rivia.

The Law of Surprise plays a critical role in the story of Geralt of Rivia. Throughout these stories, the law provides a through line of meaning and purpose in the events of Geralt's life. This custom traces its roots to a real-world Slavic tradition, invoked when a debt was owed that could not be immediately repaid. In these cases, the person performing the helping act would enact the Law of Surprise, claiming one of two prizes. The first translation of the law is "The first thing that comes to greet you when you arrive home," and the second option is "What you find at home yet don't expect." The first iteration of the law may turn out to be the guard at the gates of your home, or even a dog that comes out to meet the indebted upon their return, while the second version may mean an unexpected crop in the indebted's fields, a lover in the wife's bed, or more importantly, a child that the indebted did not know their wife was pregnant with. This is the key version of the law in the *Witcher* stories.

 ## HISTORY AND PROGRESSION

The witchers are created by taking a small child, training them, and subjecting them to a series of trials, notably the Trial of the Grasses. This trial consists of administering to the child a series of mutagenic herbs and virus cultures that modify the child's DNA. This gives them such gifts as enhanced speed and strength, at times greater vision in the dark, and extended life spans. Few children survive this process, and those who do go on to become witchers. Typically, these children are obtained through the Law of Surprise, as witchers are often in the position of providing services, and it is not uncommon for those they serve to be unable to provide payment at the time of the service. They are known as the Children of Surprise, and Geralt himself is one of them.

The scene which chronologically begins the televised *Witcher* series depicts Geralt attending a royal dinner, where he has been hired to ensure the correct suitor ends up engaged to the queen's daughter. Later in the evening, a mysterious knight arrives and claims he saved the king's life, invoking the Law of Surprise in payment. The king returned home to a newborn daughter he did not know his wife was expecting, thereby making the princess his by tradition. The knight is then forced to remove his helm, revealing himself as a creature similar to a hedgehog, and explains he has been cursed.

The queen begins to summarily deny his claim, however, the princess reveals they have been meeting in secret, and they are in love. The queen rejects this, and those other suitors in attendance join her guards in attacking the knight. Geralt responds by defending the knight and fighting alongside him. Some battle ensues, until a magical storm begins to brew inside the dining hall, and the queen commands the fighting to end. She acknowledges that there is a cosmic weight to a Law of Surprise, and to deny it may bring about awful consequences. She acquiesces to the claim, and in their love, the knight reverts to human form, his curse apparently broken. He gratefully engages Geralt, who sarcastically claims the Law of Surprise as his own reward for his assistance. As the queen reacts in horror to his use of the law, it is revealed that the princess is pregnant, previously unknown to the knight or the princess. This makes the child Geralt's tradition, setting into motion a series of events which will reshape Geralt's world.

 ## CONCEPT OF SURRENDER

Surrender is a concept which spans topics of military strategy, spiritual growth, and psychological change. Surrender is examined in religious traditions, twelve-step addiction programs, and some psychotherapeutic approaches. Some of the main tenets in each of these domains will be examined here and paired with applicable concepts in Geralt's journey.

 ## SPIRITUALITY OF SURRENDER

Nearly every religious tradition speaks of the necessity of surrender. Christianity speaks of surrendering one's inherently sinful nature to God in exchange for everlasting life and entry into Heaven. Christians are encouraged to surrender their life, decisions, and environment to God's will. In most cases, the Will of God in Christian traditions is revealed by prophets, or in the modern world bereft of such men, priests and preachers who lead the church. The phrase "surrender to the call" is often used when individuals choose to become involved in the "ministry," or take positions of leadership in the church structure. These individuals may surrender to become preachers or priests, deacons, missionaries, or youth leaders within the church. Surrender becomes the ultimate form of sacrificing one's own will and sinful human nature to the desires of God. This is considered righteous and highly honorable within the faith tradition.

Geralt is often urged to follow his "destiny" through others, many of whom he rejects outright, though his encounters with powerful beings (such as a dragon) leave him increasingly reflective of his role in the larger universe. The example often pointed to is Christianity's main prophet and icon, Jesus Christ. Prior to being arrested, tried, and crucified, Jesus is seen walking in the garden at Gethsemane praying to "let this cup pass from me." In essence, he is asking God to be allowed to go free and not be required to pay for the sins of the world through torture and death. Upon receiving no reply, Jesus accepts his fate and surrenders his own will by refusing to flee from the coming trial. Pious men of God since then have looked to follow that example and surrender their own desires and "fleshly impulses" in the services of spreading the message of Jesus and the promise of eternal salvation.

Geralt's story bears similarities to these concepts. He is given a purpose and a direction, to take in this child, however he attempts to walk away from this burden because of his own pain and worldviews. When faced with the inevitability of his path, he turns toward the pathway shown by the law and attempts to reclaim his Child of Surprise. This results in severe pain and danger for him, but he continues to follow it until he is finally granted her presence though a second claiming of the Law of Surprise, also in effect demonstrating the Christian concept of a rebirth in faith. The faith of Islam is heavily rooted in the concept of surrender as well. Islam is translated as "surrender" and Muslim as "one who is surrendered." In the Islamic tradition, writers and theologians have conceived surrender as an outward manifestation of internal love, a courageous struggle for personal growth in intensity and mastery of the universe, or as simply a child's awe of God's uniqueness. Throughout Islamic history, sects have broken away from the mainstream faith over divisions regarding the extent of surrender required by one who would call themself Muslim. Conservative groups within the faith would consider any evidence of an individual exerting their human will over the benefit of others in the community to be evidence of that individual turning their back on the prophet and the faith.

These divisions splintered the religion so frequently that eventually there was a leader by the name of Al-Hasan ibn Ali, who in his work known as the Book of Deferment sought to unify the opposing and fractured sects of Islam. He proposed that the actions of a man should not be deemed by other men as surrendered to God or not, but should instead that judgment should be deferred until the day that person dies and is judged by God. He posited that men cannot in their own journey deem others' behaviors as acceptable to God, and that God himself will make the judgment in His own time. Similarly, Geralt is often critical of others who would preach morality and righteousness, as his experiences have reinforced his opinion of humankind as inherently evil and prone to destruction. He does not hold faith in any person's ability to judge, and he often wrestles with the morality of his own decisions and whether he is even qualified to offer moral opinions.

Many people first hear of surrender in a spiritual context through the teachings of Buddhism, which speaks of the letting go of the self to allow one's true path to take shape. Buddhist practitioners seek to dissolve the boundary between self, or Atman, and the absolute, or Brahman. This requires continual surrendering of one's own preferences, aversions, and desires to better observe the elements of life and the universe unfolding without interference.

In some Buddhist traditions, the goal is to so completely remove the self from the material plane that one becomes unified with God. This is achieved through practicing nonattachment to things in the world, including material objects and even other people. Surrender in the Buddhist path is the cessation of struggle against the flow of the universe, the interruption of cosmic energies by our narratives and desires for the absence of pain at all times. Surrendering to the pain inherent in life is seen as the way to eliminate suffering within that pain.

The witcher Geralt, at the beginning of this story, is heavily invested in his concrete views of men and monsters, and his isolation and lack of connection are his defense against the despair and suffering resulting from these beliefs. His surrender comes when he turns his course and begins to seek out Ciri. This is an acceptance of the pain in his world both physical and spiritual. He ceases his resistance and suspends his ego enough to allow himself to let go of his rigid philosophies and join with the energies of the universe.

Most of these faith traditions warn against willfulness, seeing it as counter to the will of God, or the flow of the universe. Ego is seen in these traditions as the separation of self from God, and something to be sublimated to obtain greater connection with the divine and reap rewards in the afterlife. Repeatedly, the ego is seen as either base, sinful, evil, or simply a roadblock to higher purpose and functioning.

PSYCHOLOGY OF SURRENDER

Psychotherapeutic theories have also embraced surrender as a means of surmounting emotional and interpersonal struggles. Acceptance and Commitment Therapy, or ACT, embraces surrender as the action of detaching from negative or harmful narratives to accept the reality of the present moment and come into the power of our own decisions and behaviors. In therapy, the act of surrender is framed from various perspectives, however, in reality, surrender often begins the moment the individual steps into the therapy room.

It is at this point that this individual has acknowledged that their own experiences and knowledge are insufficient to attain the life they desire, and has accepted that the wisdom, perspective, or knowledge of another may hold the key to their progress. Surrender then takes the shape of submitting their own tried practices to the analysis of the therapist, and following instructions to experiment with new thought patterns, narratives, and behaviors. The individual may not necessarily surrender to the therapist themself, however the surrendering of their will and convictions to the therapeutic process of change and exploration is vital to their success.

We can entertain the absurd and humorous idea of Geralt seeking out therapeutic assistance with his life. A therapist, depending on the theoretical approach, may approach his issues from a nonjudgmental lens and avoid labeling his current decision-making process or ideologies as "bad" or "unhealthy." Instead, the focus may be on the end result of those beliefs and behaviors as they affect his life today. It would be natural to look to address the complex and chronic trauma suffered by Geralt in childhood and throughout his life. Were he to be given something like an ACES questionnaire, we would likely see the highest possible score.

Being given up by his biological parents, raised by soldiers in a ruined fort, forced to undergo the painful chemical alteration of his DNA, and exposed to violence and monsters from a young age would certainly disrupt normative development and functioning.

Assume, for the sake of this discussion, that Geralt has resolved his underlying trauma and developed appropriate trauma response mechanisms. This would leave his developmental stage conflict of reflecting on his life and legacy. Therapy may consist of encouraging Geralt to expand his awareness outside his own ego, to acknowledge the possibility that the way he sees the world may not be the only one, and indeed may not be the best. Through exploration of cause and effect, the historical results of his belief systems, and his locus of control, Geralt may begin to see the ability he has to fulfill whatever destiny is presented to him, regardless of its source. He may also be guided to see the desirable ramifications that have occurred on the occasions that he steps back from his willfulness to simply allow events to unfold. Through this process, he may begin to see the benefits of finding that peace and surrender more often, and he may begin to apply mindful strategies to bring about this surrender with increasing frequency.

The concept of surrender is also one of the central pillars of the twelve-step addiction recovery process. In Step 3, the individual is encouraged to "make a decision to turn my will and life over to the care of God as I understand Him." This is a direct action of surrendering their very life and control over to a higher power of their own conception. This is considered nonnegotiable in the recovery process, as it is believed that the individual's own willpower and willfulness have caused the addictive process to continue. In programs such as Alcoholics Anonymous, it is widely considered to be inarguable that this ongoing process of surrender is the effective path by which an individual may begin to live more in alignment with spiritual values and behaviors. Surrendering control over others, the outcomes of situations, and the very desire to use their drug of choice on a daily basis are seen as the clear path by which an individual may begin to recover from addiction. This third step, surrender, is referenced throughout the remainder of the twelve steps and continues to be a vital piece of sustained recovery.

PSYCHOLOGICAL ANALYSIS OF GERALT

The psychology of Geralt himself is of most prominence to be examined, as it is important to understand the context by which he engages with the ideals and responsibilities of the Law of Surprise. He was brought up a witcher, meaning endless combat and survival training as well as the vicious and deadly Trial of the Grasses. He has had no true childhood to speak of; instead he was imbued without his permission with supernatural abilities and tasked with seeking out and destroying the foulest, darkest monsters in the land. The better the witchers do, the less they are needed, and over the decades they come to be seen as monsters themselves.

Strange and dangerous, society begins to reject and shun them, unless they are in desperate need of the services of a witcher. This path leads to Geralt living alone in a sort of exile, yet compelled to seek out monsters to make a living. He also seems to provoke bigots and ignorant folk whenever he can, seeming to be seeking acceptance though he knows how unlikely this is. Additionally, Geralt is reportedly somewhere around one hundred years old. Typically, in the human lifespan, experiences are processed through the lens of an aging body, a changing relationship to our environment, values, and goals. The stages of development as presented by Erikson clearly define various conflicts that must resolve throughout an individual's life to create emotional and psychological health.

According to Erikson, Geralt would be in Stage 8: ego integrity vs. despair. This stage consists of an individual reflecting on their life. They begin to look back on the things they did or did not accomplish to determine whether they feel fulfilled. Geralt has encountered endless streams of dark and dangerous monsters, all while enduring the rejection and revilement of fellow humans. Though he may be able to acknowledge his successes in battle, his life may seem the same as it ever was, with Geralt traveling alone, outcast and with no legacy to indicate he ever existed.

This likely leads to a sense of hopelessness and a lack of faith in any kind of guiding force in the universe. His life has become one of self-will, moving him forcefully from one task to the next without anyone to answer to or find true comfort in. It is this despair and cynicism which leads Geralt to mock the Law of Surprise, and also fuels his irreverence for kings and queens, and indeed even the claim that humans are preferable to monsters in most cases. This insight also breeds positive behaviors, for Geralt is a deep thinker, seeing truth in deception and complexity where others prefer black and white. His despair is paired with a flicker of hope within him that the world might become a better place somehow. This leads to compassion for the creatures some would call monsters, and swift retribution for "civilized" humans who perpetrate cruelty and malice. Geralt's worldview in that sense is achieved through supreme self-reliance, further distancing him from concepts of destiny and true purpose. This brings us to the conflict of surrender vs. willfulness.

SURRENDER APPLIED TO *THE WITCHER*

A multisystem understanding of surrender is best used to analyze the cosmic events at play in the *Witcher* story, and Geralt's responses to them. Within the story, the Law of Surprise acts as a god of sorts, an abstract universal will, guiding and shaping events in the world according to some intelligence or predetermined pattern. It is clear in the stories that refusal to abide by the Law of Surprise results in some level of pain and suffering not only in the life of an individual but in the world overall. The storyline hints that the refusal to take the Child of Surprise has resulted in a series of decisions and interactions that have caused nations to go to war, resulting in conflict and transcontinental chaos.

Ciri, the Child of Surprise, has some powers that the rulers in Nilfgaard are keen to possess. Geralt's fulfillment of the tradition would have brought her anonymity as a witcher, thereby turning the attention of these rulers away. Notably, Geralt does attempt to claim the law when he begins understanding the power of the tradition, but he is imprisoned instead when Ciri's grandmother, the queen, decides she will not allow Ciri to return with Geralt. As Geralt begins pursuit of Ciri, events in the world begin to sway back toward peace.

It is understandable, given what is known of the witcher Geralt, that he would resist sublimating his own identity to attain unity with the universe and its cosmic events. Geralt's own ego has been wounded by the stripping away of his identity and forced involvement in the monster hunters. He would be fiercely protective of his own internal narratives regarding his personal values and belief systems, seeing them as the only expression of control he can maintain in a world that both despises and desperately needs him. His experiences with the cruelty of men and abuse of power from the ruling elite would further turn him away from a belief in benevolent power and a caring, intelligent universe.

It is evident that Geralt comes to sympathize with many creatures that others would consider monstrous, while showing his contempt for humans at almost every turn. On the surface, he seems to be wandering the world, seeking something strong enough to kill him. Yet through the events of his story and life, we come to see he is seeking something deeper still, though most of the time this search seems to be subconscious and reflexive. He takes up with Jaskier, who by any account would cause Geralt misery with his positive disposition, optimism, and constant noise-making. Despite this, something new emerges in Geralt, almost a deep yearning to connect. It may be this very connection that Geralt is seeking when he decides to turn back to claim Ciri, and indeed it could be behind his eventual desire to seek his destiny.

Geralt slowly opens himself up over time to accepting connection, friendship, and even trust in others. His begrudging friendship with Jaskier is supplemented with his complicated emotional tie to Yennefer, the sorceress. They meet many times, and the attraction between them is undeniable. However, because of their backgrounds, suspicions, and trauma, they struggle to trust the bond between them. These relationships seem to soften his hardened shell of cynicism and survivalist thought processes. This allows him to consider the benefits of surrendering his firmly rooted core beliefs to accept the path of the universe, represented here by the Law of Surprise.

Throughout the events of the *Witcher* saga, Geralt's plans and preferences continue to be supplanted by the needs or requests of others, increasingly showing him the possibilities of accepting other perspectives and ideologies. He is increasingly being introduced to small acts of surrender, allowing events to take shape without his direct influence, or to unfold in spite of his attempts to control them.

CONCLUSION

At the conclusion of the first part of the *Witcher* story, the clear and direct results of surrender for Geralt become evident. He elects to help a farmer who is surrounded by monsters in the forest, and Geralt is badly wounded. In his weakened state, he puts his fate in the hands of the farmer, who takes him home to tend his wounds. Lying in the home, awaiting care, the door opens and Ciri comes into the room. The farmer's wife, unknown to him, has found Ciri and taken her in while he was away. Through an ultimate act of surrender, Geralt has found his way back into the flow of the universe, and he is united with Ciri, his Child of Surprise.

The story of Geralt may be the reflection of many individuals throughout time. Humanity has been trying since the dawn of time to understand the greater forces at work around it. Storms, luck, emotions, and faith have all been used by humankind to create the gods, the representations of all man cannot comprehend. While humanity attempts to formalize and define higher powers, there is an inherent disconnection from the essential flow of events in time. This leads to an imposition of will on our environment, an assumption of control over uncontrollable forces. The ensuing struggle leads to incongruent beliefs and behaviors, ultimately causing cognitive dissonance. The various philosophies, spiritual perspectives, and psychological theories discussed here are a living blueprint of humanity's attempts to find its way back to a state of stillness and peace.

About The Author:

BRIAN ADAMS is a Licensed Marriage and Family Therapist in California, about an hour south of Sacramento. Brian works in an intensive outpatient program during the week for a major health care organization, specializing in treatment of high-risk individuals in crisis. On the weekends, Brian runs therapeutic Dungeons and Dragons sessions for at risk youth in a group home setting. Brian is a certified Therapeutic Game Master, and loves to incorporate unique and innovative interventions to explore role playing as a therapeutic tool. DUring off days, Brian enjoys playing games with his two children and wife, and relaxing with his dogs, Charlie, Sunny and Ditto.

References

Cherry, MsEd, K. (2022). *Erikson's Stages of Development.* Verywell Mind. https://www.verywellmind.com/erik-eriksons-stages-of-psychosocial-development-2795740

Greyber, D. (2011). Practicing the Art of Surrender. *Rosh Hashanah*, 1(5772).

Nygard, M. (1996). The Muslim Concept of Surrender to God. *International Journal of Frontier Missions*, 13(3).

Preece, R. (2007). *The Solace of Surrender*. Tricycle. https://tricycle.org/magazine/solace-surrender/#:~:text=Buddhism%20asks%20us%20to%20relinquish,nature%20that%20is%20transforming%20us.

Smith, C. (2023). What it Means to Surrender to God. *Open the Bible*. https://openthebible.org/article/what-it-means-to-surrender-to-god/

Tiebout, MD, H. (n.d.). *The Act of Surrender in the Therapeutic Process*. Silkworth.net. https://silkworth.net/alcoholics-anonymous/the-act-of-surrender-in-therapeutic-process/

2

GERALT AS A MASCULINE CONSTRUCT: WHEN THE ONLY THINGS THAT ARE TOXIC ARE THE POTIONS

MELISSA HUNTLEY AND CASSANDRA BUCK

"You don't need mutations to strip men of their humanity. I've seen plenty of examples."

— Geralt of Rivia, *The Witcher 3*

The lands of the Continent are filled with supernatural violence, and the ones charged with resolving it are the witchers. Ruthlessly trained and brutally transformed, witchers become supernatural beings themselves—dogged and aggressive defenders of the land and its inhabitants, for the right price. With Geralt acting as our proxy, we are invited to experience their extreme lethality, inhuman strength, and fierce courage via books, video games, and television. Though the witcher class seems to illustrate the kind of intense virility designed to fuel the ultimate male power fantasy often associated with toxic masculinity, Geralt of Rivia's characterization contradicts and, at times, outright undermines this.

The concept of "toxic masculinity" was initially introduced by Shepherd Bliss in the late twentieth century as a way to identify how certain traits commonly displayed in hypermasculine culture actually worked against men's well-being. However, it wasn't until the 2010s that the term entered public discourse more fully, particularly in the context in which it is now often used—that is, as traits often implicated in the manifestation and normalization of aggression and brutality, including sexual assaults and domestic violence.

At the center of toxic masculinity is the overall idea that strength through physical domination and the repression of emotions is the cultural ideal of a man. The effects of this internalized attitude are as numerous as they are destructive: rampant and violent homophobia which leads to Nilfgaardian-level codes of conduct to perform straightness; sexism and misogyny and ultimately normalized brutality against women; emotional distance and isolation to the point where a complete lack of engagement in family life is seen as a standard, if not humorous, paternal role—all of which are punctuated with a generous side of violence in the name of defending and upholding an unrelenting and distorted idea of manhood.

The implications of this on men and on society as a whole are calamitous, with the resulting pressure of scripted masculine ideals intersecting with increased rates of domestic and sexual violence, as well as increased instances of substance abuse, depression, and violent death among men. It is for this reason that representations of healthy masculinity in mainstream media are crucial. And with games like *Witcher 3* selling over 50 million copies, it is even more vital that nourishing characterizations of masculine role models like Geralt are made visible. But what is it about Geralt, and in some cases, the Witcherverse, that lends itself to the subversion of the damaging discourse of toxic masculinity? And what makes it effective?

Geralt's characterization offers a counterbalance to multiple cornerstones of the toxic masculine constructs. Despite his outwardly strong and tough appearance, the White Wolf transcends the tropes of toxic masculinity by sustaining emotional bonds and intimacy with male friends such as Jaskier. Moreover, he leaves behind toxic masculine expectations of dominance and power over women in his primary female relationships, such as with Yennefer and Ciri. The outcome is a strong, healthy representation of masculinity which is readily accessible and consumed via various media channels.

GERALT AND DANDELION: THE NOT SO LONE WOLF

Whether you know him as the Jaskier of the original Polish stories and Netflix show, or the Dandelion of the English books and CD Projeckt Red's video games, there is little doubt that both the bard and his relationship with Geralt hold a special place in the hearts of fans. Though aspects of Jaskier and Geralt's relationship in the video game and television series diverge from the original novels, the essence of their bond remains more or less the same; theirs is a meaningful platonic companionship rooted in the kind of physical and emotional intimacy that is often obstructed by the barriers of toxic masculine constructs such as homophobia. Fans of the Netflix series are made to understand this bond explicitly in Season 1, Episode 4, when Jaskier helps a very naked Geralt with his ablutions in preparation for an important royal social event.

Despite what Henry Cavill fans may think, the intent of this scene is not to provide the audience with some fan service—well, maybe just a little. Rather, it serves to convince the audience of the closeness of Jaskier and Geralt's bond. Where Geralt's grumbling assertions seem an attempt to convince both him and the audience that he and Jaskier aren't actually friends, Jaskier rather comedically calls his bluff by reminding him that only moments before he had "rubbed chamomile on [his] lovely bottom." The comedic tone of this exchange belies the significance of the scene, which is underscored moments later when the dialogue takes a more somber turn. Geralt tells Jaskier, "I need no one. And the last thing I need is someone needing me." And Jaskier replies, "And yet, here we are."

Geralt and Jaskier share an attachment that lies outside the bounds of what more prohibitive standards of traditional masculinity allow for. This in turn creates space for physical intimacy. This physical intimacy is demonstrated repeatedly in the books with examples including the two characters sharing clothes and Jaskier clasping Geralt's waist as they ride horseback together. Their connection is not limited to physical familiarity. Rather, we are treated to glimpses of their emotional intimacy as well. An example of this can be seen in the first chapter of *Blood of Elves*, in the confrontation of Jaskier by Geralt's infamous on-again, off-again love, Yennefer.

> "How did it go? 'Her heart, as though a jewel, adorned her neck. Hard as if of diamond made, and as a diamond so unfeeling, sharper than obsidian, cutting—' Did you make that up yourself? Or perhaps . . . ?"
>
> Her lips quivered, twisted.
>
> " . . . or perhaps you listened to someone's confidences and grievances?"

From this exchange, readers come to understand that Geralt has shared his and Yennefer's thorny emotional affairs with Jaskier, thus proving his status as Geralt's confidant in matters of the heart. Despite his outwardly appearance, we know that Geralt does not prescribe to stereotypical (and at times, toxic) rules of masculinity, which often preclude emotional and physical intimacy with other men. Though toxic masculine constructs would have us believe that emotional vulnerability and physical intimacy are signs of weakness, it is demonstrated time and again that Geralt's emotional openness and physical connection with Jaskier does nothing to undermine his masculinity.

In all the critiques of the Netflix series, nowhere is there commentary on Henry Cavill's depiction of Geralt as "unmanly" or unconvincing as the—let's call a spade a spade here—absolute badass that he is. Moreover, demonstrations of the free and easy intimacy between Jaskier and Geralt in the books do not erode the reader's experience of Geralt as a compelling, strong male character. Never do we see Geralt's masculinity subverted or questioned. Instead, Geralt and Jaskier demonstrate elements of physical and emotional intimacy in their friendship in a way that turns tropes of toxic masculinity on their head and, in turn, models healthy male friendships to readers, players, and viewers alike. Players of the video game do not wonder at the feebleness of the character they play. Rather, they are invited to enjoy the extravagant fight scenes of a seasoned warrior as well as his passionate sexual interludes.

GERALT AND ROMANCE: THE MASCULINE FEMINIST

Geralt's healthy intimate connections are not limited to tagalong bards. The expectation of highly masculine traits as toxic may lead to the assumption that Geralt, as a hypermasculine witcher in a historical fantasy setting, might approach women from a place of misogyny. He certainly is not wanting for romantic partners throughout his many adventures. And while the world of the Continent overall has quite a harsh and anti-female approach to how the women are treated, Geralt has strikingly different views on the treatment of the opposite sex.

Despite the prevalence of gender-based violence and chauvinism in the background and context of his stories, Geralt shows none of these tendencies, treating both short and long-term romantic partners with the same respect that he affords everyone. Though Geralt is presented with many romantic options in his quests, the one we see him most active and emotionally invested in is Yennefer of Vengerburg.

Yennefer is a powerful sorceress who is fiercely ambitious and takes no flack from others, witchers or otherwise. She is headstrong and speaks her mind, acting in her own interests more often than not. In spite of (or due to) this, Geralt finds their paths entwined at many crossroads. At no point does he belittle Yennefer and her chaotic motivations. Rather, he clearly respects their differences. He shows that he is fully aware of her character upon finding her in *The Witcher 3*, wherein she immediately summons him to meet with the Emperor of Nilfgaard under the guise of a compelling lead, saying, "Must have been a damn good offer. Not many things you'd give up your freedom for, and even fewer people."

Here Geralt shows that he understands and accepts her fierce independence, not only giving credence to their current conversation of dealing with the emperor, but also implying that this is not the first time their own relationship has been in conflict with her need for freedom. Geralt stands beside Yennefer as she struggles with her own romantic feelings, particularly in her mistrust of their relationship and her suspicions that they remain tied due to Geralt's wish of a djinn that their two fates be connected. At no point does Geralt attempt to control or manipulate her into staying by his side, accepting that both of them will find what they need in a partner.

He also does not put Yennefer on a pedestal but accepts her as a fully three-dimensional, flawed person. He defends her character to others while acknowledging her often problematic actions, saying, "I'm not about to justify what Yennefer did, but try to understand her. She's not doing this to anger you. She's doing this for Ciri."

The White Wolf accepts her feelings and expressions of pain and uncertainty, without judgment or derision of "female emotions," confident in her ability to come to the conclusion that suits her best, even when it means her sudden absence or silence on important matters. The unhealthy way for Geralt to deal with this could be attempting to control Yennefer and demanding answers or even her unwavering attention and priority under the guise of "loyalty" once the relationship begins. This entitlement to a romantic partner's agency is a well-known toxic trait and is a serious sign of an unsafe relationship for both parties.

Completely opposite to this dangerous mind frame of relationships, players of the video game can even have Geralt fully confront Yennefer about her imperial attitude and unnecessary secrets and lack of communication:

> "The guys . . . Well, they're not exactly happy with you. Because . . . you aren't willing to say what you're planning. You're treating them like pages, not including them—us, actually, 'cause I feel that way too."

In this dialogue, Geralt does not delegate or distance the feelings to "the guys." He owns his own emotions and tells Yennefer exactly how he feels he has been mistreated, allowing her to understand and process his point of view. In subsequent scenes of Uma's trial, we see Yennefer make an effort to be more polite and open with Geralt and the other witchers.

Players can even have Geralt take the initiative to express his own vulnerability in regard to his own capture and escape from the previous game, *The Witcher 2: Assassins of Kings*. Geralt asks Yen, "Why didn't you look for me after you'd recovered your memory and your freedom?" She replies, "I assumed you would recover quickly and find me first." And he responds, "You had mages to help you, I was on my own."

Contrary to popular archetype, Geralt is clearly communicating that he was in a dangerous place and hinting that he could have greatly benefited from Yennefer's presence, while arguing against her stereotype of the "lone wolf" witcher being strong enough to need no one. It is clear from this conversation that Geralt feels comfortable asking after his own emotional needs in their relationship, something that goes largely hidden in discussion around stereotypically masculine romantic partners.

GERALT AND CIRI: DAD OF ~~DESTINY~~ DETERMINATION

"It's hard to regret something you didn't choose."

— Geralt of Rivia

One of the biggest storylines in all versions of *The Witcher* is the relationship between Geralt and his Child of Surprise: Cirilla of Cintra. While the books and television series focus on the origin and growth of their relationship, nothing delves into the White Wolf's role as a father more than the video game *The Witcher 3: Wild Hunt*, where the entire story revolves around Geralt first finding the missing adult Ciri, then guiding her through her destiny in his role as her father.

On the surface, Geralt's initial interactions with Ciri appear to fit the trope of the unwitting and unwilling single father figure. In return for saving the life of Duny, Urcheon of Erlenwald, Geralt flippantly claims the Law of Surprise and asks for "something he has but does not yet know," leading to the record-scratch moment of learning Duny's wife is pregnant just minutes later. Geralt immediately flees this paternal duty, as he has no desire to raise a child, and expresses frustration at the bad taste fate has in fostering children. However, as Geralt says, "people linked by destiny will always find each other."

He eventually meets Ciri as a young girl and immediately sets off on the journey of trying to hand the responsibility to someone else he deems a more appropriate parent, first Yennefer with the reasoning that Ciri will need help with her magic, and then his own father figure Vesemir, under the guise of keeping her safe at the fortress Kaer Morhen. So far, Geralt's relationship with Ciri reflects only the burden of fatherhood and his attempts to avoid the responsibility result in the common trope of a reluctant gruff older man leading a plucky young female ward through their world of violence.

However, Geralt forgoes this simplistic portrayal of fatherhood as he begins to train Ciri in the ways of witchers. He sees her potential as a warrior and a powerful magic-user and personally addresses this with her. What is most significant lies beyond sword practice and monster hunting lessons: Geralt emotionally connects with Ciri as he raises her, speaking openly about the mental difficulties of her situation. He blatantly dispels the falsehood of unfeeling witchers in *Blood of Elves* and Season 2, Episode 5, "Turn Your Back." Ciri says "I want to be like you, Geralt. I want to be indifferent to the past. To the lies. To the things I've done. Please. Let me have that," to which Geralt replies, "To be neutral does not mean to be indifferent or insensitive. You don't have to kill your feelings. It's enough to kill hatred within yourself."

As Ciri grows and learns from her violent war-torn surroundings, he reminds her of the burden of taking lives in *Sword of Destiny*:

> It is easy to kill with a bow, girl. How easy it is to release the bowstring and think, it is not I, it is the arrow. The blood of that boy is not on my hands. The arrow killed him, not I. But the arrow does not dream anything in the night.

At the beginning of Season 2, in "A Grain of Truth," he listens to Ciri express her trauma and frustration around it and guides her through processing her thoughts and emotions in a supportive manner, rather than encouraging her to toxically repress her feelings, saying, "Fear is an illness. If you catch it and you leave it untreated, it can consume you. You face it. Facing your fear is not easy. But I am here for you. I won't let anything happen to you."

When the White Wolf steps with intention fully into the role of fatherhood, he fulfills conventionally masculine duties of protecting and providing while expressly meeting her emotional needs. This is most clearly seen at the end of *Witcher 3*, where the player, as Geralt, is charged with the task of advising a now adult Ciri as she prepares to stop the White Frost, a cataclysmic event that threatens not just the Continent, but the world beyond.

In a game where the vast majority of the gameplay is based on fighting and violence, it is telling that what determines the outcome of the story is the player's choice in how Geralt interacts with Ciri. If they choose to have Geralt react to his daughter's needs in an overly protective and possessive manner, like insisting on accompanying her to strategic discussions, or to dismiss her concerns out of hand, such as encouraging her to drown her worries in a cup of ale, it results in a tragedy for Ciri and the story at large.

But if the player chooses to guide Ciri toward independence and maturity by helping her to accept and express her frustrations through connections and vulnerability, whether it be an impromptu snowball fight or trashing old furniture, and if the player chooses to show confidence in her ability to handle important political moves on her own, then Geralt, as her father, has given her tools to stand strong in the face of extreme adversity. As Geralt says, "A dynasty can't survive on arrogance alone." It is clear that in this story, a successful father's legacy is one that is not centered on the father figure itself, in how men can shape and guide the next generation through emotional maturity and trust in others.

In this way, Geralt vastly transcends the one-dimensional portrayal of toxic masculinity characteristic of violence-prone witchers. This behavior isn't unique to Geralt. Several other witchers show nurturing tendencies as well, welcoming Ciri to Kaer Morhen and taking part in raising her. "Uncle" Vesemir makes her clothes to train in, and the other members of the School of the Wolf guide her in her journey. Above all, Geralt and the witchers do not hide from these familial bonds behind the guise of gruff aloofness, and they are proud of what the Lion Cub of Cintra means to them, in the aptly named eighth episode of Season 2, "Family." Geralt tells Ciri, "I know you're afraid, Ciri, but what you see in there, it isn't real. We belong together. You, us, it's not perfect, but it is real. It's yours. We are your family . . . and we need you."

 WITCHERS AND THE WIDER WORLD

People . . . like to invent monsters and monstrosities.
Then they seem less monstrous themselves.

— Geralt of Rivia, *The Last Wish*

Geralt and the witchers at large show highly masculine healthy characteristics in a world beset by violence and danger. Despite the homophobia that is expected from such men, Jaskier is Geralt's closest and dearest friend. In a setting where violence toward women and lack of female agency are commonplace, Geralt intentionally seeks out partnerships with powerful women who challenge him at every turn, and he engages intimately with only the most enthusiastic of consent, regardless of social standing or relationship status. And despite all the tenets of toxic masculinity focused on emotional repression, he remains unequivocally open to his daughter, successfully shifting the narrative of the story and his own legacy to the next generation: the ultimate goal of fatherhood.

Through Geralt and the rest of the witchers from the School of the Wolf, readers, watchers, and players alike become very familiar with healthy expressions of strong masculinity. Role models like these grant people who want to be masculine a constructive example, one that is not toxic to the self or others but rather encourages clear expressions of connections with other people in a myriad of different contexts. Recognizing that toxic masculinity is just one subset of characteristics of the much larger gender role reduces sexism against all masculine traits and can create healthy expectations of what men and male characters can bring to personal connections.

The witchers have shed the arbitrary, dangerous limitations put on male and masculine characters. Through this we can not only see how limited certain tropes can be, but also become more aware of the nuances and intricacies of the people in the world at large. The witchers invite us all to heartily toss a coin to and embrace the monster slayers of the world who come home to hang up the sword and then emotionally connect with their loved ones, to give and receive support in a harsh world, and to ultimately and unabashedly be the most unfettered version of themselves.

About the Authors

MELISSA HUNTLEY is a lecturer at the University of Shimane in Hamada, Shimane of Japan. She earned her bachelor's degree in psychology at Buena Vista University and her master's in TESOL at Southeast Missouri University. Her research focuses on cross-cultural psychology between Japan and the United States. She encourages readers to read her other chapters in The Psychology of Zelda, The Psychology of Final Fantasy, and The Psychology of Pokemon. In the Lands Between, she lives on the Dodge button.

CASSANDRA BUCK hails from the sunny Sonoran Desert in Tucson, Arizona. She studied anthropology with a focus on gendered linguistics at the University of Arizona and received her Master's in archaeology from the University of Oxford. When she is not reading, writing, or talking about the ancient dead, she enjoys gaming, traveling, and a well-poured pint. Her favorite character in the *Witcher* universe is the stuffed unicorn.

References

Addis, M.E., & Mahalik, J.R. (2003). Men, masculinity, and the contexts of help seeking. The American psychologist, 58 1, 5–14 .

Askey, B. (2018). "I'd rather have no brains and two balls": Eunuchs, masculinity, and power in Game of Thrones. The Journal of Popular Culture, 51 (1), 50 – 67.

Bem, S. (1974). "The Measurement of Psychological Androgyny." Journal of Consulting and Clinical Psychology, 42 155–62.

Brown, J. F. (Executive Producer). (2019–2021). The Witcher [TV series]. Netflix.

Gross, D. (1990). Toxic masculinity and other male troubles—the gender rap. The New Republic., 202(16), 11–14. https://doi.org/info:doi/

Harrington, C. (2021). What is "Toxic Masculinity" and Why Does it Matter? Men and Masculinities, 24(2), 345–352. https://doi.org/10.1177/1097184X20943254

McGinley, A. C. (2018). The masculinity motivation. Stanford Law Review Online, 71, 49 – 59.

Pittman, F. S. (1993). Man enough: Fathers, sons, and the search for masculinity. New York: Putnam.

Salter, A., & Blodgett, B. (2017). Toxic geek masculinity in media: Sexism, trolling, and identity policing. Springer.

Sapkowski. (2007–2018) The Witcher Saga. Hachette

Sapkowski. (2016). The Witcher Video game Series. Warner Bros Interactive Entertainment.

3

BROTHERHOOD KNOWS NO BOUNDS, ONLY BONDS

ABBIGAIL POLLACK

"Fear Is An Illness. If You Leave It Untreated,
It Can Consume You."

— Geralt

A witcher is defined as "someone who has undergone extensive training, ruthless mental and physical conditioning, and mysterious rituals in preparation for becoming a hunter," not far from our military's preparation. While in the novels, comics, games, and lore, fewer than a hundred witchers are able to conquer their trials and training, the United States military has around 1.4 million active-duty personnel. Despite the vast difference in numbers, *The Witcher* and the military share one typical mentality: identity and camaraderie are critical in the face of any adversity. This chapter examines parallels between the warrior group witchers and real-life elite military servicemembers' bonds of brotherhood in the face of grief and loss following post-9/11 eras of war; precisely, how the development and strength of camaraderie can shape the response to bereavement, trauma, and moral injury faced by soldiers since the early 2000s.

The *Witcher* Netflix series, games, literature, lore, and even tabletop role-playing games highlight the concept of brotherhood, the formulation of identity, and development of skill sets. Similar topics resonate with popular psychological theorists including Erik Erikson and George Vaillant. Through the lenses offered by these theorists, we will compare the lore of The *Witcher* and real-life examples of the US military, taking an in-depth look at the cultural formation of an individual and their relationship within a group, and potential outcomes for mental health. By pulling in quotes and citations from the *Witcher* series and excerpts from servicemembers stories, readers may be able to envision the experiences without needing to have enlisted or stepped foot on the Continent.

Finally, this chapter investigates the role of social interaction and brotherhood in mental health interventions for loss and grief, examining the mental health outcomes for individuals who have formed a solidified bond under shared directives and extreme circumstances after a traumatic event and subsequent grief, and how the themes of brotherhood and a sense of identity are fostered and sometimes threatened in the face of traumatic events.

BECOMING A WITCHER AND A WARRIOR

"People . . . like to invent monsters and monstrosities.
Then they seem less monstrous themselves."

— Geralt of Rivia, *The Last Wish*

Before diving into the outcomes of the Brotherhood, it is crucial to recognize the foundation and history of these warrior groups, starting with the witchers. The lore of *The Witcher* can be experienced through the video game and animated series. In it, witchers are created to help humanity survive against monsters who have invaded the land for nearly three centuries. Following the Conjunction of the Spheres, beings across the universe are able to access other spheres, invading and spreading to them. As the human population increases on the Continent, they face the terror of being hunted by newly invading apex predators. Humanity's solution to this rising issue begins by using another recent invader, the Chaos, also known as magic. Harnessing the power of the Chaos, mages become a dominant force in protecting humanity, but it is still not enough. The mages take to the Castle of Reisberg to develop and train warriors with both magical and physical skills. Through their experiments, they determine that only children are mentally and physically capable of surviving the transformation into witchers. Orphaned children are trained in combat to test their physical limits and mental fortitude. The intensity of the training is shown by the number of children falling ill or dying. Of note, in the lore, females who engage in the experiments die almost instantly. Five male children survive the first experiments. These warriors become known as witchers and develop a fearsome and formidable reputation throughout the Continent. Under the instruction of a knight, the mutated warriors take on the values of duty, honor, and purpose. After completing their training, the Brotherhood establishes their Order of the *Witcher* in Castle Morgraig, coming together with a sense of purpose and duty under a collective code.

Mages continue experimenting on children to increase the witchers' number, honing their process to specific trials and tests. In the first, The Trial of the Grasses, children are injected with alchemical potions and viruses to alter their bodies and minds; many die during this phase, sometimes only ten percent completing it. Those who succeed develop increased strength and agility with decreased aging. The next obstacle is the Trial of the Dreams, in which, children are given visions to increase their mental fortitude and enhance their general abilities. Last, the Trials of the Mountain, seen as a final exam, comprises challenges set by trainers to test all candidates' newly enhanced abilities and survival skills. On completion, candidates are given their medallions and welcomed into the Order of the *Witcher*. Graduated witchers may take contracts to fight monsters through the spring and fall. They return to Castle Morgraig in the winter to honor those who have died and gather with those still living.

Unrest develops among the witchers, leading to many members leaving the Brotherhood and starting their own schools. The first group to depart is the Order of the Bear, later known as the School of the Bear, which offers a different training program for witchers. Over time, other schools develop their own creeds, values, codes, and purpose. In addition to the School of the Bear, we find the School of the Cat, the School of the Griffin, the School of the Manticore, the School of the Crane, the School of the Viper, and last, the School of the Wolf. The Order of the Wolf, the last remaining group in Castle Morgraig, later settle in the Kaer Morhen valley following an attack on all witchers throughout the land. A survivor of this, and graduate of the School of the Wolf, is Geralt of Rivia.

SCHOOLS OF WAR

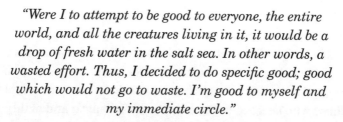

"Were I to attempt to be good to everyone, the entire world, and all the creatures living in it, it would be a drop of fresh water in the salt sea. In other words, a wasted effort. Thus, I decided to do specific good; good which would not go to waste. I'm good to myself and my immediate circle."

— Zoltan, *Baptism of Fire.*

While our own world may not have magic, mages, or colliding spheres, we do have warriors trained through challenges meant to push the limits of mental abilities and physicality. General service members from the army, navy, marines, air force, space force, and coast guard are trained in cohort-style boot camps to build strength, endurance, character, and integrity, and to foster a sense of purpose for their mission and future career. Many service members become bonded over tests to push their limits and mental capabilities. It is upon completion of their training that newly graduated service members join smaller units of teams to serve and protect.

Like the world of *The Witcher*, there are smaller splintered groups of elite warriors with different values, duties, purposes, and trials meant to develop soldiers with unique skills for any threat. While the witchers call them schools, the military calls them special operations teams, each with expertise and skill sets that parallel those of the factions on the Continent. In the original novels, there are three canon witcher schools: the Wolf, the Cat, and the Griffin. The tabletop role-playing game and video games add four more schools: the Bear, the Viper, the Manticore, and the Crane. Their real-world military equivalents are the Navy SEALs, Army Rangers, Marine Raiders, and Air Force Combat Controllers. Though many try to join their ranks, only an elite few succeed.

 ## THE ARMY RANGERS

Much like the witchers, candidates for the Army Rangers face trials and obstacles, put in place to increase strength, skill, and purpose within their units, fostering brotherhood and camaraderie throughout the process. Army Rangers complete three one-week phases of intense training in three different regions of the United States. In the first phase, the number of candidates is cut by nearly half, as many soldiers need help completing the first week's physical or mental training portion. The second phase consists of leadership and combat training, obstacle courses, and team training, all while being pushed to their physical limits with minimal sleep and food. In the last phase, soldiers are airdropped into the training area, where they must hone their water survival skills. Once they graduate, they move on to their units with other Army Rangers. Of note for this topic on camaraderie, the first line of the Ranger creed is "Never shall I fail my comrades."

As one of the most popular specialty military teams, the Army Rangers are most closely akin to the School of the Wolf, home to fan favorites Geralt of Rivia and Vesemir. The School of the Wolf is the most well-known and longest lasting of the schools. Its members are known for their reliability and well-rounded physical and alchemistic combat training.

THE NAVY SEALS

Since their formation in 1962, the Navy SEALs have been one of the most well-known groups of elite soldiers. In order to become a SEAL, candidates must pass a physical screening test. The Navy SEAL school takes longer than the Rangers, requiring fifty-eight weeks from start to completion. During the first eight weeks, soldiers are given multiple physical screenings. Failure to pass the final test means being recategorized into a different role in the navy. If an individual completes the eight-week physical course, they move on to the next phase known as BUD/S (Basic Underwater Demolition SEAL training), a twenty-four-week training course on developing mental and physical stamina alongside leadership skills. During this phase, they must complete Hell Week, a grueling five and a half straight days of physical conditioning on fewer than four hours of sleep. Roughly 25 percent of candidates succeed. They continue to train in land, air, and sea warfare.

Next, candidates undergo another twenty-six weeks of training, known as SEAL Qualification Training, to hone their skills. After graduation, the new SEALs join platoons. The code by which a Navy SEAL lives includes values such as loyalty, honor, heritage, courage, discipline, respect, and excellence.

There are clear overlaps between the SEALs and the *Witcher* schools, particularly the School of the Crane, located along the shore of the Continent. The Cranes appear in the collection *Tales from the World of the Witcher*, written by other fantasy writers, though they are briefly mentioned in the video games. Though not much is known about the school as it is rarely mentioned, we are told that the School of the Crane specializes in slaying monsters of the land, air, and sea. Sound familiar? Other schools specialize in general land monsters with few aquatic creatures. Those under the Cranes train and fight against demons of the rivers, lakes, and seas. Much like the SEALs, the Cranes are as comfortable in the water as they are on land, if not more so.

THE MARINE RAIDERS

The Marine Raiders (whose motto, Spiritus Invictus, means "Unconquerable Spirit") are the elite fighting group reactivated in 2006 from the marines, known as MARSOC until 2015. The first phase of their three-week selection process starts with a twenty-thre-day training phase meant to identify the candidates most likely to succeed in the next phase of training. Phase one is focused heavily on physical capabilities, pushing the body and mind to new limits. Candidates then attend a nine-month training course which focused on building strength, agility, and mental stamina through continuous operations and team tactics, with limited sleep. The final phase in the training consists of obstacles and challenges meant to address all previously developed skills along with assessing team strength, dynamics, and their ability to work together. Upon completion, service members are sent on a final six-month training course. By graduation, nearly 75 percent of individuals have dropped out. *The Witcher* equivalent of the Raiders would be those who train under the School of the Bear. Depicted only in the video games, graduates of the School of the Bear are known for their strength and stamina above all else. Unlike the Raiders, the Bears are more likely to be independent and autonomous. Heavily armored and even more heavily equipped, the School of the Bear is thought to be one of the strongest and most formidable of the schools. Their endurance and strength are unmatched by any other branch or school.

THE AIR FORCE COMBAT CONTROLLERS

Last, the Combat Controllers are highly trained operators in the US Air Force. One member obtained the first Medal of Honor ever recorded. Combat Controllers are assigned to battlefield areas and create and operate air zones for air support. Members are often embedded in other special forces teams like the Army Rangers and Navy SEALs. The selection process for becoming a Combat Controller takes up to two years, with only about 90–95 percent of candidates being selected. A candidate requires high physical test scores to move to the second phase, where they continue to be tested on stamina and endurance on land, sea, and air. Upon graduation, many Combat Controllers are assigned to other special force units, including the Army Rangers and SEAL Teams.

Combat Controllers rely heavily on their strategy, cognition, and intuition to plan and create the defensive air zones. There are two witcher schools that deploy similar strategies: the School of the Griffin and the School of the Manticore. The School of the Griffin was mentioned in *The Lady of the Lake* and further fleshed out in the video games and TTRPG. Like the Combat Controllers, the School of the Griffin values preparedness and mental flexibility. The Griffin's graduates are able to adapt into different social circles, similar to the Controllers, who are able to integrate flawlessly into SEAL and Ranger teams. In a similar vein, the School of the Manticore is also represented in the Controllers' strategies. The School of the Manticore, introduced as well in the video game and TTRPG, is a smaller school located in the east, near the desert. The Manticores prioritize defense and the science of creating potions, relying heavily on their wits and ability to think quickly and strategically—skills no doubt also found in Controllers, as they use the lay of the land for supporting airfields and air support.

Other witcher schools include the Cat and Viper. The School of the Cat is one of the original groups in the *Witcher* saga with little equivalent in the military world. A Cat medallion is flaunted by Leo Bonhart in the series, and later retrieved by Ciri and worn throughout training. The School of the Cat relies heavily on the agility and stealth of its pupils, who excel as assassins and rogues with a strong proclivity for bloodlust. The other honorable mention, the School of the Viper, appears in the video game series. These witchers are more ruthless than other schools, accepting bounties for not only monsters but humans as well. Many gamers may recognize the school for its connection to one of its graduates, the assassin Letho of Gulet, featured in *The Witcher 2*.

Much like in the world of *The Witcher*, special operations teams are often smaller schools of highly trained individuals meant to fight any known threat for the protection of others. Whether a member is part of the general service or one of these groups, they often are placed into high-stakes, high-threat environments, where their skills and reliance on each other are tested to meet a particular goal. During war or conflict, many soldiers are lost to the service of protection, leaving behind the weight of grief at their loss for those remaining unit members. Many remaining service members may experience post-traumatic stress as a result of near loss of their own lives or as a moral injury from an act against their moral code, such as the loss of another. Regardless of how hard an individual trains or practices, losses are a part of war. How do the bonds created through teamwork and shared goals or purpose help to mend those wounds, whether you are fighting monsters foreign, domestic, or otherworldly?

PSYCHOLOGICAL LENSES OF CAMARADERIE

"No one wants to suffer. But yet it is our lot. And some suffer more. Not necessarily by choice. The point is not the bearing of suffering. The point is how it is borne."

— Ciri, *The Tower of Swallows.*

Brotherhood and camaraderie in the Kaer Morhen are a focal point for most of the second season of *The Witcher* on Netflix, focusing on those members in the School of the Wolf, from newcomer Ciri attempting to join the elite fighting force to the life-and-death decisions made against a person's moral standing after an accident that threatens the entire group. Spoiler warnings throughout the chapter for those who may have yet to watch the show, read the books or comics or played video games.

In the Netflix series, Geralt and Ciri travel back to Kaer Morhen to seek refuge in the mountains, as Ciri is wanted by many. Kaer Morhen is a haven and home to witchers, the School of the Wolf's birthplace and base throughout the winter. This is where viewers of the show have their first real taste of what it takes to become a monster hunter, as well as the kinship developed for those who survive the process. Throughout the season, tension builds between Geralt, Vesemir, the group leader, and Eskel, one of the younger witchers who appear injured following a monster fight. As the injury festers, Eskel becomes more withdrawn from the group, exhibiting changes in behavior and eventually forming into a monster that no brother can recognize. At the same time, Ciri is starting her training and building strength within herself, gaining the attention and approval of others in the Order. This gives viewers a chance to see the relationships formed through the process and the hard work needed to pass any obstacle in a witcher's way. The entire season is an excellent example of identity development for various characters, as well as what can happen if an individual is "less successful" with one stage and how that may have a ripple effect on those around them.

THE WORLD OF ERIK ERIKSON

When considering an individual's place in the world and how they relate to others, it is essential to consider the stages of development needed to become who they are in the context of their world. Erik Erikson devised a theory of psychological development and personality. He organized this development into stages. Many of his stages begin in early childhood, though the entirety of the theory spans until the end of life. In discussing identity and role development in groups with the context of both the military and *The*

Witcher, we will begin with the fourth stage in the theory: Industry vs. Inferiority. This stage may be more pertinent when discussing the witcher's development as it explores the late childhood to early teen years. In this stage, children are immersed in education, training, and cognitive development, with a significant emphasis on modeling coming from teachers. In this stage, we would find Ciri from the first season of *The Witcher* on Netflix. Throughout the season, viewers are shown the character attempting to live up to the expectations of being royalty and learning to develop her survival skills while on the run from Nilfgaard. A witcher's training and skills are developed through practice under a master in that skill. During this time, children are seen having more complex and driven social relationships, and they start developing peer groups. In the case of *The Witcher*, this is when most individual bonds are formed with overall emphasis on the bond to their school. This stage can also be seen in the second season, as Ciri begins training to become a witcher, learning from those around her and forming peer groups among the other witchers. Success in this stage is often seen as competence over a skill, so long as the child survives the challenges themselves. As a result of this stage, children begin to believe in their ability to handle themselves and look out for each other through their increased sense of competence.

The next stage relevant when discussing warrior development is the identity vs. role confusion stage of Erikson's theory, taking place between the ages of twelve and eighteen. This is the first stage where relevant beliefs can be developed for real-world military members, as enlistment can begin as early as seventeen. In this stage, the mind and body are changed based on new opportunities and skills which provide chances for the exploration of belief systems, goals, and values while they search for individual identity and sense of self. Near the end of this stage, individuals start to consider their place in society, including their career, friends, family, and community. Erikson states that this fifth psychosocial stage exists "between the morality learned by the child and the ethics to be developed by the adult." Seasons two and three of the Netflix series illustrate this stage very well with Ciri, as she explores her abilities and role in the larger Witcherverse. In Season 2 we see her developing her skills as a future witcher and finding her place among the Order, completing training regimens and obstacle courses. The third season is where it turns into this stage's morality piece. Ciri learns that she can see the futures of individuals, particularly when they are going to die, and argues with Yennefer about the morality of not telling someone about their later demise. Later in the season, Ciri is forced to question that sense of self when she is shown visions of previous family members, exacerbating her doubts about herself and her abilities.

Upon successfully completing these stages, warriors in either world would have a greater sense of themselves and their role in the universe. Many service members are part of a unit, a group of soldiers with various responsibilities formed to meet one greater goal or mission. An individual who has successfully understood their capabilities and role within their unit would be able to foster positive relationships within the team. One military service member described this as "our whole adult life is combat books and a rifle, part of this huge culture that's full of purpose and passion." Over time, the sense of trust and that the other members in the unit are also successful in understanding their role or capability will develop. In the case of *The Witcher*, this may mean an understanding that members of the Order are as skilled and knowledgeable as each other and able to hunt and fulfill contracts with success, ensuring the maintenance of the Order. In this stage, the role of brotherhood and kinship plays a pivotal role in maintaining a sense of success and purpose, a protective factor against grief and loss.

When faced with that grief or loss, witchers and soldiers alike may question their sense of self and revisit the previous stages or be unsuccessful in the next Erikson stage, Intimacy vs. Isolation. Changing their sense of self and questioning abilities following a loss may cause an individual to be "unsuccessful" in previous stages and thus not successful in this stage. If an individual is seen as unsuccessful in this stage, they will often become increasingly isolated and withdrawn from others. This is well illustrated in the scenes showing isolation, avoidance, or withdrawal, which are often key symptoms in both post-traumatic stress disorder and moral injury, leading to increased emotional distress. Camaraderie in these situations is most important when examining the longer-term effects of grief and loss. Humans (and mutated humans) are social creatures with better socioemotional safety in groups. Being isolated in this stage of development can lead to being unsuccessful in other stages, eventually leading to feelings of being unproductive in the world and fear of being unable to accomplish what an individual set out to do. Camaraderie in the face of adversity can soothe the effects of grief and loss, increasing a sense of purpose or value and causing individuals to move away from growing isolation.

GEORGE VAILLANT'S THEORY OF ADULT DEVELOPMENT

George Vaillant is another theorist to consider when examining the warrior ethos and identity development. He believed an individual's identity developed across six significant stages in life: developing an identity, development of intimacy, career consolidation, generativity, becoming a keeper of the meaning, and achieving integrity. Vaillant's theory can be examined through various *Witcher* storylines in the series, video games, books, and comics. The first stage, developing an identity, occurs in childhood, when individuals separate from their parents, creating their values, passions, and beliefs. The best example of this is Ciri in the series, or the children in the comics.

The next stage, the development of intimacy, is where individuals begin to have a reciprocal relationship with another person, recognizing that their sense of self can include another person (this does not limit itself to intimate relationships). Many military members recognize this stage while training or reciting their creed upon graduation. If a traumatic loss occurs in this stage of identity development, an individual may lose their sense of self or deny future availability to others, increasing isolation. In career consolidation, an individual turns their task into a lifelong commitment or service after graduation, in the military or witcher schools. Loss in this stage may mean an individual questions their career choice and may leave their service. Having a sense of brotherhood or service to others in this stage may mean the success of future roles for both that individual and the collective in the next stage.

The generativity and guardianship/keeper of the meaning stage is where an individual wishes to foster or guide the next generation and continue the culture. An example is Vesemir at the conclusion of the animated series. Last, the integrity stage is where an individual comes to terms with their past near the end of life. By adding the sense of kinship and camaraderie while looking through the lenses of Vaillant, a warrior developing their sense of purpose may identify more protective factors and have an easier chance of developing these areas of identity. Those without a sense of partnership may not continue to pursue their values or goals and would not likely continue to pass down traditions and culture to future generations, thus ending a warrior culture and ethos.

BUILDING BONDS

"Anxiety is never irrational, Geralt thought to himself,
aside from psychological disturbances. It was one of
the first things novice witchers were taught. It is good
to feel fear. If you feel fear, it means there is something
to be feared, so be vigilant. Fear does not have to be
overcome. Just don't yield to it.
And you can learn from it."

— Geralt, *Season of Storms*

The newest generation of military service members, the post-9/11 cohort, is among the largest in military and veteran history, with eighteen million veterans and twenty-one million active-duty and reserve members. Studies have shown that roughly three-quarters of veterans have deployed at least once and were twice as likely to have served in a combat zone. Nearly half of all post-9/11 veterans have reported emotionally traumatic and distressing experiences related to their military service, with one-third seeking mental health assistance. Two of the most common disorders being treated within the VA are post-traumatic stress disorder (PTSD) and depression. Both diagnoses are also highly correlated with the loss of another or grief over lost abilities an individual may have once had. The rate of depression among soldiers is five times as high as that of the civilian population, and rates of PTSD are almost 15 percent higher. Studies have indicated that approximately 14 to 16 percent of US service members meet the criteria for PTSD or depression. Recent studies have also shown that more than thirty thousand active-duty personnel and veterans have died by suicide since 2001, which is four times higher than those killed in war operations.

Grief and loss pose a significant physical and psychological risk to individuals impacted by the pain. Studies have shown that risk factors related to complicated or long-standing grief include depression, anxiety, poor physical health, and lowered perceived social support. Most risk factors listed would be the opposite of what we would expect in a warrior culture built on the foundation of kinship. Most behavioral interventions for grief and loss support lessening negative cognitions and avoidant behaviors through increased social support. Other research on bereavement has shown more significant levels of resilience during the grieving process in individuals who have a more favorable view of the support they can expect from others, as well as their ability to rely more on their support systems, openly share their thoughts, and have less worry about available support when needed.

Events that challenge a sense of ability or purpose laced with grief and loss may negatively impact individuals, leading to higher levels of emotional distress from increased social isolation and withdrawal. The elite training of military service members, especially those in special forces divisions, may imbue an inherent sense of camaraderie due to sheer smaller cohort sizes, so to encourage this in larger military structures, interventions have been developed. Much like Geralt and Ciri in the comics and video games, the US military has implemented a battle buddy program, in which your battle buddy can help both in and out of combat to decrease that possible desire for isolation. The battle buddy program was designed to lower the risk of suicide among military members but also to reduce negative mental health consequences in times of distress. The program has been shown to reduce rates of suicide among military members, promote cooperative problem-solving, increase general morale and confidence, decrease stress, and improve safety in training and combat.

ENDINGS WHICH ARE BEGINNINGS

Overall, the Witcherverse is a beautiful illustration of the sacrifice needed to become a warrior, but more than that, the shared desire to be a part of something with a shared goal, to protect. This chapter hoped to shed light on the strength and fortitude of soldiers and their brotherhoods in the real world, and in fantasy, to become the ones who stare back into the void. One of the initial questions we have posed relates to the mental health outcomes for individuals who have formed a solidified bond under shared directives and extreme circumstances after a traumatic event and subsequent grief. Bonds created during these hardships and trials are meant to help foster growth and, in a way, fight back against the threats that may be more psychological. Many servicemembers have strong ties to those they met in bootcamp or in the specialty schools. It is not far-fetched to imagine the camaraderie these smaller groups have when you consider the brotherhood that can be seen with the overarching branches. Just ask any military member their thoughts on the Army vs. Navy football game. Through the works of Erikson and Vaillant, we are able to recognize where threats of grief and loss may emerge and how they can plague a person's identity and social relationships in the future. Following a traumatic event, a person may have the instinctive desire to withdraw, to isolate from others. This is a critical component of both PTSD and depression, which are often found in the military population. A service member may go through something that threatens their life or their moral code, so they may try and stick to themselves or in the barracks instead of going to the chow hall or physical training. Through the lens of Erikson and Vaillant, a person may question their sense of self or their purpose in the world, and without positive social supports, these can lead to increases in depression, grief, or loss. Longer-term isolation from a unit has the potential to decrease unit cohesion, trust, or more importantly, preparedness. However, consider that same individual turning toward their unit, using the others as an exercise to strengthen their feelings of support. Cognitive Behavioral Therapy calls this method of participating in something you may not want to as Behavioral Activation.

Which leads to the other initial question: how are themes of brotherhood and a sense of identity sometimes threatened in the face of traumatic events? Humans (and likely mutated fantasy humans) are social creatures and are meant to create groups and support other for survival. When an event occurs where survival is not achieved, that may lead to second-guessing competency and potential withdrawal from others, increasing likelihood of mental health distress. During a time of crisis, where a person questions themself and their abilities, a sense of kinship and brotherhood with those around who have experienced similar concerns can lead to more positive mental health outcomes. Many military members often talk about loss in the battlefield, the loss of a friend, a buddy, a civilian, a leader, or even someone they never knew apart from their shared uniform. These stories make mention of thoughts such as *What could I have done differently?* or *That could have been me*, or even *That should have been me*. When service members have the opportunity to discuss those thoughts with others or find individuals who had those same thoughts once, improvements in overall mental health can be found. Current military programs have been set into place to increase the opportunity for bonds to be built throughout a warrior's story and even after they decide to hang up their helmets. Through brotherhood and relationships, a person can feel more equipped to accept their own grief or loss as a part of themselves. Much like the *Witcher* saga, every warrior's story is open-ended, to be remembered and recalled not only about themselves, but about those who were impacted by their presence.

"Never lost. Always found"

About the Author

DR. ABBI POLLACK is a clinical psychologist in Dallas, Texas. Abbi works on the Primary Care Mental Health Integration team at the North Texas VA, connecting veterans to mental health services both inside the VA and in the community. Often as a veteran's first experience with mental health, Abbi likes to incorporate movies, TV shows, comics, and pop culture references to make treatment feel more engaging and comfortable for those new to treatment. Abbi has a clinical interest in Moral Injury and Post-trumatic Stress Disorders with hopes of incorporating both table top and video game role-playing games as potential treatment interventions with veteran populations. When not at work, Abbi likes spending time with her wife and cats, playing video games or Dungeons and Dragons, and reading comic books.

References:

CD PROJEKT RED. (2015). *The Witcher® 3: Wild Hunt* [Video game].

Chongruksa, D., Prinyapol, P., Sawatsri, S., & Pansomboon, C. (2015). *Integrated group counselling to enhance mental health and resilience of Thai army rangers.* Asia Pacific Journal of Counselling and Psychotherapy, 6(1–2), 41–57.

Cooper, A. D., Warner, S. G., Rivera, A. C., Rull, R. P., Adler, A. B., Faix, D. J., . . . & Millennium Cohort Study Team. (2020). *Mental health, physical health, and health-related behaviors of US Army Special Forces.* Plos one, 15(6), e0233560.

Erikson, E. H. (1980). *Identity and the life cycle.* W W Norton & Co.

Everly, G., McCormack, D., & Strouse, D. (2012). *Seven characteristics of highly resilient people: Insights from Navy SEALs to the 'Greatest Generation.'* International Journal of Emergency Mental Health, 14(2), 137–143.

Ghahramanlou-Holloway, M., LaCroix, J. M., Koss, K., Perera, K. U., Rowan, A., VanSickle, M. R., . . . & Trieu, T. H. (2018). *Outpatient mental health treatment utilization and military career impact in the United States Marine Corps.* International journal of environmental research and public health, 15(4), 828.

Ghazal, S. S. (2022). *An Assessment of Resilience and Wellness of the Canadian Rangers* (Doctoral dissertation, Carleton University).

Heritage, F. (2022). *Magical women: Representations of female characters in the* Witcher *video game series.* Discourse, Context & Media, 49, 100627.

Kennedy, C. H., & Zillmer, E. A. (Eds.). (2022). *Military psychology: Clinical and operational applications.* Guilford Publications.

Koenig, H. G., Youssef, N. A., & Pearce, M. (2019). *Assessment of moral injury in veterans and active-duty military personnel with PTSD: A review.* Frontiers in psychiatry, 10, 443.

Ledford, A. K., Dixon, D., Luning, C. R., Martin, B. J., Miles, P. C., Beckner, M., . . . & Nindl, B. C. (2020). *Psychological and physiological predictors of resilience in Navy SEAL training.* Behavioral Medicine, 46(3–4), 290–301.

Levin-Rector, A., Hourani, L. L., Van Dorn, R. A., Bray, R. M., Stander, V. A., Cartwright, J. K., . . . & Lattimore, P. K. (2018). *Predictors of post-traumatic stress disorder, anxiety disorders, depressive disorders, and any mental health condition among US Soldiers and Marines, 2001–2011.* Journal of traumatic stress, 31(4), 568–578.

Molendijk, T., Kramer, E. H., & Verweij, D. (2018). *Moral aspects of "moral injury": Analyzing conceptualizations on the role of morality in military trauma.* Journal of Military Ethics, 17(1), 36–53.

Nindl, B. C., Barnes, B. R., Alemany, J. A., Frykman, P. N., Shippee, R. L., & Friedl, K. E. (2007). *Physiological consequences of US Army Rpanger training.* Medicine & Science in sports & exercise, 39(8), 1380–1387.

Richardson, N. M., Lamson, A. L., Smith, M., Eagan, S. M., Zvonkovic, A. M., & Jensen, J. (2020). *Defining moral injury among military populations: A systematic review.* Journal of Traumatic Stress, 33(4), 575–586.

Roberts, B. M., Mantua, J., Naylor, J. A., & Ritland, B. M. (2023). *A narrative review of performance and health research in US Army*

Rangers. Journal of strength and conditioning research, 37(5), 1157–1161.

Sapkowski, A., & French, D. (. (2014). *Baptism of fire*. First US edition. New York, NY, Orbit.

Sapkowski, A., & French, D. (. (2017). *The lady of the lake*. First US edition. New York, NY, Orbit.

Sapkowski, A., & French, D. (. (2016). *The tower of swallows*. First US edition. New York, Orbit, an imprint of Hachette Book Group.

Sapkowski, A., & French, D. (. (2018). *Season of storms*. First US edition. New York, Orbit.

Sapkowski, A., & French, D. (. (2015). *Sword of destiny*. First US paperback edition. New York, NY, Orbit.

Sapkowski, A., & French, D. (. (2013). *The time of contempt*. First US edition. New York, NY, Orbit.

Sapkowski, A., & Stok, D. (2017). *Blood of elves*. First trade paperback edition. New York, Orbit.

Sapkowski, A., & Stok, D. (2019). *The last wish: introducing the Witcher*. First hardcover edition. New York, NY, Orbit.

Sharkey, J. M., & Rennix, C. P. (2011). *Assessment of changes in mental health conditions among sailors and marines during postdeployment phase*. Military medicine, 176(8), 915–921.

Smith, E. N., Young, M. D., & Crum, A. J. (2020). *Stress, mindsets, and success in Navy SEALs special warfare training*. Frontiers in psychology, 10, 2962.

Vaillant, G. E. (1992). *Ego mechanisms of defense: a guide for clinicians and researchers*. American Psychiatric Pub.

4

"WAIT—WHO ARE WE SUPPOSED TO BE FIGHTING?" REHUMANIZATION IN *THE WITCHER*

ALEX BAKER

"It is easy to kill with a bow, girl. How easy it is to release the bowstring and think, it is not I, it is the arrow. The blood of that boy is not on my hands. The arrow killed him, not I. But the arrow does not dream anything in the night. May you dream nothing in the night either."

— Geralt, Sword of Destiny by Andrzej Sapkowski

I n real life, using violence against another is never a decision to be made without first considering all other alternatives. The emotion of guilt has been an evolutionary tool that helped create reluctance toward harming others, allowing us to maintain difficult relationships and cohabitate in peace. Perpetrators of violence often lack this empathy or have trained themselves to minimize the suffering of others. By emphasizing the perceived wrongdoings of their victim, we have felt justified in treating them as less than human.

Following the countless and tragic examples of killing unarmed Black individuals, arguments have often been made to put the victim's character into question. During legal hearings of the officers involved, a history of using marijuana, shoplifting, or other misdemeanor offenses is often unearthed, as if this justifies the lethal force used against them. In doing so, human life is treated as conditional, condoning capital punishment based on arbitrary information. As people are not treated with human dignity, polarization of our society has reached an all-time high.

The world of *The Witcher* shows a frightening parallel to many unthinkable behaviors in human history, set in a more digestible fantasy context. Looking for anchoring points in a chaotic environment, we may naturally want to be told who is good and who is bad. However, just like reality, *The Witcher* does not afford us this luxury of being able to categorize creatures so easily. Each of us is susceptible to influences around us and capable of both helping as well as hurting. The charismatic leader may sin far more than the grotesque monster. To better understand how people make decisions that end up brutalizing one another, it helps to first understand *why* we allow ourselves to do this.

DEHUMANIZATION

"Hatred and prejudice will never be eradicated. And witch hunts will never be about witches. To have a scapegoat—that's the key."

– Geralt, *Witcher 3: Wild Hunt*

Humans have always categorized each other in terms of good (our side) and bad (the other side), whether in terms of social cliques, sports teams, religion, ethnicity, or military decisions. Social psychologist Jonathan Haidt notes that this concept of tribalism has had an adaptive purpose throughout our evolution, helping us both to "bind and blind." By creating clear distinctions of ally and enemy, we have a quick way of finding those we sit with and those we jeer at. Student athletes often describe the visitor team as repugnant during any home game. Opposing military generals each believe that God is on their side before a battle. While our evolutionary emphasis on teams, competition, and allegiances has helped to increase feelings of connectedness with "our" people, this separation also creates an extreme outgroup bias against everyone else not on our team. We may minimize the positive contributions by those different from us while emphasizing our own self-righteousness.

In order to reinforce our egocentric beliefs that ours is the best team to be on, we often invalidate, demean, or make others out to be somehow less than human. As psychologist Leon Festinger describes, people experience cognitive dissonance when there is a disconnect between our behaviors and our beliefs. If I experience guilt and remorse when I hurt others, then I either need to A) avoid hurting them or B) justify to myself why they deserve to be hurt.

This process of dehumanization, or taking away the aspects that make others "human," has been used for the most unthinkable atrocities throughout time to justify our wrongdoings. It is far more acceptable to stomp on an insect than to kill a human. Most nations have at some point used media influences to encourage others to look down on other nationalities, religious groups, political beliefs, and skin colors. They describe their enemies as subhuman, comparable to weasels, apes, vermin, cockroaches, or other creatures. By temporarily muting the voice in our head that says we cannot harm someone we consider like ourselves, human beings have been responsible for the holocaust, slavery, terrorism, as well as all other forms of xenophobia and systemic racism. Although we would like to think of video games as a fantasy world separate from human experiences, sometimes this echo into our lives is what makes them so powerful an example of teaching us important lessons.

The Witcher offers a framework for how to stand against xenophobia, model empathy, and promote advocacy toward repairing ruptures between those from vastly different backgrounds. Like countless other RPGs (role-playing games), *The Witcher* places the hero in the role of slaying monsters for coin, experience points, or quest completion. However, the dichotomous lines between friend and foe are frequently blurred into a morally ambiguous gray zone. Players frequently wonder whether they made the "right decision" about how they resolved each conflict, despite the lack of perfect outcomes. More so than any other video game series to date, *The Witcher* forces players to confront some uncomfortable realities about the backgrounds of who they must kill. This discomfort is intentional, creating a moment of perspective-taking and reverence toward the lives of others, despite being so different. Characters from *The Witcher* books, TV shows, and game franchise often become enveloped in high-stakes dilemmas involving right and wrong. While this can be done through adept writing and character creation, the physical platforms used for storytelling greatly influence how immersive and realistic they become. To understand how morality in video games has changed over time, we first need to understand the history of RPGs.

HISTORY OF VIDEO GAMES

While the name *"Akalabeth: World of Doom"* probably doesn't mean much to most, *Akalabeth* was one of the first RPG games with a visual aspect, shaping our paradigms about heroism and monster-slaying. Designed by high-school student Richard Garriott in 1980, *Akalabeth* transformed the world of paper and pencil games into an immersive experience that allowed their hero to fight skeletons, orcs, gremlins, and demons. Behind a screen, players could take on the role of the fabled hero that saves the world and achieves glory through a linear goal of conquering bad guys and getting stronger. Video games of that era created a clear distinction of who the enemy was, with little convoluted backstory to obscure your mission of killing them.

As RPGs have evolved over time, video games continue to set clear expectations by placing you as the saintly champion of good. Most other inhuman-looking NPCs (non-player characters) are evil loot-piñatas created for your exploitation, gold, and experience. As part of the process of leveling up, saving the world, and becoming more powerful, you're often assigned various kill or fetch quests that involve killing X number of unnamed ghouls, bandits, or goblins. This is such a common occurrence that the term "grinding" was coined specifically to describe destroying as many enemies as efficiently as possible, often waiting at the place where they first come into existence to immediately eviscerate them and complain about how long it takes for them respawn.

While butchering multitudes of highly pixelated skeletons in *Akalabeth* didn't give the player any cause for concern, over forty years of graphics improvements have made this fantasy violence feel more malicious. Stanley Milgram's social psychology research from the 1960s put participants in the uncomfortable position of being a disciplinary teacher, punishing pupils through electric shocks. The study explored obedience, including the participant's willingness to say no when given an order to hurt someone who supposedly deserved it. His study revealed that people feel less discomfort hurting others the more physically or emotionally distant they feel from their victim. It is much easier to hurt someone when you know less about them, do not feel directly responsible, and can avoid their suffering. While slain enemies simply disappeared in early 8-bit platforms (think Obi Wan Kenobi from *Star Wars: A New Hope*), modern systems like the PlayStation 5 have added extensive layers of immersive and emotionally draining carnage after each creature kill. As it becomes harder to tell whether a character is an ally or enemy, the player begins to experience more uncertainty, discomfort, and hesitation about whether they are justified in using violence. The better that video game graphics become, the more guilt the player experiences in dehumanizing their enemies. As technology and game engines continue to evolve, it becomes more difficult to separate fantasy, artificial intelligence, and humanity.

In 1970, a Japanese roboticist named Masahiro Mori coined the term "Uncanny Valley" as "the phenomenon whereby a computer-generated figure or humanoid robot bearing a near identical resemblance to a human being arouses a sense of unease or revulsion in the person viewing it." Masahiro could not have anticipated how much technology would change in the next fifty years, leading to a revolutionary change in how people discern what is real and what is fake. In *Witcher 3: Wild Hunt*, players can see far more nuanced changes in NPCs, including pain when they are injured, sorrow when they regret an action, or joy when they are left to interact with their preferred environments. Tears can be seen in vampires following guilt for their behaviors. Watching the target of your contract play with his family leaves you feeling genuine empathy toward them, rather than simply a source of experience points. A combination of technological advances for gaming platforms and expert character writing have resulted in feeling wholly part of the character's world, reducing the disconnect and arbitrary lines dividing "us" and "them." Just like Milgram's study related to harming others, forcing players to feel directly responsible for the harm they cause makes them question the necessity of their actions. By putting people physically and emotionally "up close and personal" with their victims, the dehumanization begins to dissolve.

REHUMANIZATION

"Nations are invisible lines that people assign meaning to. A life, however. A life has real meaning. It's warm skin and a beating heart. It should only be taken as a last resort. Righteousness can easily become rage. Justice can easily become scorn."

— Geralt, *The Witcher*, Season 3 Episode 4: "The Invitation"

While many psychologists have spoken to the horrors of dehumanization, the reverse concept of "rehumanization" has been less frequently been addressed. As dehumanization involves removing the human elements from others by treating them as an object that cannot feel pain, rehumanization relates to highlighting the relatable characteristics that make people feel a sense of kindship with others. Instead of actively working to degrade others as being undeserving of life, rehumanization fosters the bonds between people and sharing in their pain.

Neuropsychological research has shown biological structures and brain regions involved in dehumanization of others. Psychologists Susan Fiske and Mary Wheeler identified brain regions related to feelings of guilt necessary to rewire the brain to feel compassion for those they wrong. Some individuals may naturally be more averse and sensitive toward hurting others (empaths) while others on the opposing extreme may be more callous and unemotional.

Although no one enjoys the feeling of shame and embarrassment after wrongdoing, this emotion teaches us to prioritize compassion through avoiding unnecessary violence. Ongoing research in these brain regions can help to teach us how to rehumanize and build in care for those we wrong.

Rwandan genocide survivor and advocate, Hyppolite Ntigurirwa, emphasized the need for empathy in the process of rehumanization. Perpetrators of mass violence are often conditioned to separate themselves from personal accountability, imagining their victims as faceless, nameless, and nothing more than barriers that stand between themselves and their goals. By retraining individuals to lean into the innate feelings of understanding and compassion, by pausing to see others as multifaceted, complex, and recognizing similarities within us, we no longer see them as animalistic or devoid of the intrinsic value of life.

The world of *The Witcher* creates a microcosm of opportunities to decide how you would handle problems involving humans and monsters. Throughout your quests in *The Witcher*, you uncover the rich history of your suspects and determine what you have in common before making the decision to draw your sword. Some suspects feel easier to dispose of, while others cause our moral compass to go haywire. While you can certainly take a "slash first, ask questions later" approach to the game through dehumanizing all your enemies, your conscience may feel heavier when acting solely because someone told you to do so. Ultimately the decisions you make toward different monsters of *The Witcher* universe may give you an opportunity to rehumanize others. Whether or not that process translates into your real life is up to you.

MONSTERS OF *THE WITCHER*

"The next few minutes passed in a recital of the monsters which plagued the local peasants with their dishonorable doings, or their simple existence."

— *The Last Wish*

The main protagonist of *The Witcher* series is the sullen Geralt of Rivia, a mercenary swordsman commissioned by local townsfolk and nobility alike to exterminate the unwanted creatures of the Continent. Witchers are magic-imbued beings created through a series of rigorous trials and biological engineering to increase physical potency, recovery, lifespan, and disease resistance. Through a combination of sword fighting, magic, potions, and impeccable detective skills, Geralt executes contracts to destroy various forms of beast, monster, and monstrosity. Luckily, the world is rich with a diverse array of basilisks, bruxas, wraiths, and other monsters for Geralt to hunt.

As his professional title of "witcher" suggests, Geralt's role alludes to the witch hunts of systematically dehumanizing and annihilating those believed to be responsible for the maleficence in their communities. While many history records show that twenty-five people died in the 1692 witch trials of Salem, Massachusetts, not one witch was actually killed. Witches had only started to exist when the local government needed a diversion and target to blame for difficulties related to colonizing their "new world." Similarly, local leaders in *The Witcher* often hire Geralt to eradicate dissenters or quirky individuals they do not understand. Through his witch-hunting duties, Geralt too must decide whether the contract-issuer or the target is truly guilty.

Through *The Witcher* show and game series, some creatures are unequivocally evil, and no tears are shed when slain. As the four-armed grave hag known as "Mourntart" digs up graves and kidnaps children, Geralt has no moral qualms about ending her ways. There are certainly creatures with no sense of remorse or reason that cannot be humanized. However, far more of the creatures from *The Witcher* come with murky, tragic, and conflicted backgrounds that require Geralt to consider their motivations.

Striga

When King Foltest's daughter is transformed into the burly, ghoulish banshee known as a striga, he looks for Geralt's help reversing the curse without destroying his beloved child. The princess/striga is described as "slimy, black, twisted, and dragging a tentacle-like umbilical cord behind it." Despite the vicious blows inflicted on him by her claws, Geralt reminds himself that the creature is acting not out of spite but through self-protective instincts related to the curse imposed on it. While many other adventurers and even witchers have attempted the king's seemingly impossible quest, only Geralt is able to show both empathy and sharp-thinking needed to help subdue and return the princess to her original self. He is able to see in the striga the human elements of emotional reactivity and being trapped in unfortunate circumstances not of your own doing.

Succubus

After a group of town guards go missing, Geralt follows their trail to find a succubus named Salma. Succubi look like human women with hooves and tails, surviving based on their need to drain the energy from men. When confronted, Salma acknowledges that she is responsible for the guards' deaths. However, she also points out that she was attacked and caught off guard, leading to her efforts to protect herself. Geralt's decision places him in a modern-day example of victim-blaming, ignoring the context that compelled the woman toward self-defense. This example highlights how many of the creatures Geralt must encounter have indeed acted aggressively, though there is often a provocateur and reason for the behavior.

In a later quest, Geralt tracks down a forest succubus that is accused of stockpiling rare alchemy reagents for sinister purposes. When confronted about the hoards of flowers in her home, she says, "What do you think they're for? They're pretty! Monsters have aesthetic preferences too, you know." Who doesn't want a matching outfit or a little bit of home decoration? While monsters may be dangerous and can be violent when pushed, they may also have wants, needs, and everyday preferences. By taking the time to talk with these succubi, Geralt is able to see human traits of appreciating the unique beauty found in life.

Wraiths

During one of the earliest *Witcher 3: Wild Hunt* quests, Geralt hunts a noonwraith haunting a well. A noonwraith is a banshee without a lower jaw, wearing a tattered spectral dress reflective of her last living day. As Geralt explores relevant leads to her purpose and history, he discovers the noonwraith was a bride-to-be who was hanged in a well for daring to try and escape a tyrannical estate lord. She lingers on and haunts the well, only hoping to find a treasured bracelet given to her by her betrothed. While Geralt ultimately frees her spirit from this world, his understanding of her past allows him to show her pity rather than loathing. He was able to see in the noonwraith the human traits of love, attachment, and being the victim of another's jealousy.

While helping a prince named Olgierd escape a pact he made with a deity, Geralt discovers the man's sordid past. After his early life as a gangster, Olgierd married Iris and moved her into his manor. Over time, Olgierd's demonic pact left him devoid of love, resulting in him murdering Iris's father and discarding her to waste away the rest of her short-lived days in captivity. Now her spirit remains bound to the manor, painting her fondest memories of when she was still in love with Olgierd. As Geralt relives Iris's marital turmoil through her frighteningly realistic canvases, he builds compassion for the ghost haunting the manor. She is torn between an existential dilemma: being bound to the manor for eternity or ceasing to exist entirely. While Geralt helps her to finally make the right decision, this journey pulls at his heartstrings, pushing him want to hold Olgierd responsible for the pain he caused his spectral bride. Geralt is able to see in Iris the human traits of tragic love, subjecting yourself to pain in order to also feel an intimate connection.

Godlings

A wealthy merchant buys property in town and commissions Geralt to get rid of the noises coming from within, by any means necessary. Geralt discovers a docile and playful godling named Sarah squatting in the basement of the home. Godlings are child-looking nymphs who are protective of their environment and tend to be mischievous. Sarah befriended a magical dreamer that lived in the home, seeking companionship rather than causing harm to anyone. Rather than chase Sarah out, Geralt recognizes her dilemma and deceives the merchant into cutting his financial losses and abandoning the property, ultimately creating a haven for Sarah to reside in. By doing so, Geralt prioritizes Sarah's basic needs over the merchant's wealth. He is able to see in the godling the human need to survive and find connection in a world that abhors and rejects you.

Trolls

When local silver miners ambitiously found a cave in their search of ore deposits, they realized that they entered the home of Wham-a-Wham, a rock troll living among the silver deposits. Rather than immediately attacking, he kindly asks them to leave. When the miners ignore his request and begin dismantling his home in search of profit, Wham-a-Wham is forced to stand his ground and stop the miners. Although contracted to kill the troll to avenge the ambitious miners, Geralt is able to empathize with the beast's story and find peace through leaving him alone in his cave.

As Geralt and his pugnacious witcher pal Lambert ascend a sacred mountain, they are met by a tribe of mountain trolls who ask them to leave their weapons behind before they approach the summit. While Lambert encourages cutting the trolls down for daring to make such a request, Geralt complies and is able to prevent unnecessary bloodshed. Geralt is able to show humility toward the trolls, respecting their wishes, preserving lives, while still completing his quest. He is able to see in the trolls the human traits of culture, reverence toward the sacred, and attempting to find win-win solutions rather than resorting immediately to violence.

Werewolf

When Geralt is tasked with ousting a werewolf by the name of Morkvarg from a holy garden, he is prepared for a simple monster battle. However, the task becomes more complex as he learns that the werewolf was once a vicious pirate that was cursed with an eternal hunger that no meal could ever satisfy. As Morkvarg knows that killing him will only leave his immortal-self trapped in the curse, the werewolf begs Geralt to free him from his misery. Geralt is then left with difficult decision regarding whether to break the curse, as well as whether to vanquish Morkvarg for the monstrous deeds he did as a human. Although no clearly correct decision is available, Geralt is forced to reconcile the complexities of whether Morkvarg is a man, a monster, or somewhere in between. He is able to see in the werewolf the human trait of remorse for his actions, as well as the desire to be free from his pain.

Vampire

After a series of high-profile murders within her empire, a vampire princess commissions Geralt to hunt down and eliminate the creature responsible. Throughout his journey, Geralt uncovers the culprit, Dettlaff, an honor-driven vampire noble. Geralt's tracking efforts leave him one step behind Dettlaff in the continued slayings. However, a series of clues reveals that Dettlaff is being blackmailed to kill these royal individuals in order to avoid his kidnapped love's demise. The twist? Dettlaff's love, Syanna, is the one orchestrating the blackmail the whole time, using herself as leverage to get him to kill those who have wronged her. She was abused throughout her childhood and cannot stand the thought of her perpetrators getting away. Ultimately, Geralt realizes that no one's hands are clean and continued bloodshed will not wipe away the sins of the past, urging them all toward a future armistice. He is able to see in Dettlaff the human side of sacrificing your values to protect those who mean most to you.

 NONHUMANS

"People like to invent monsters and monstrosities. Then they seem less monstrous themselves. When they get blind-drunk, cheat, steal, beat their wives, starve an old woman, when they kill a trapped fox with an axe or

middle the last existing unicorn with arrows, they like
to think that the Bane entering cottages at daybreak is
more monstrous than they are. They feel better then.
They find it easier to live."

— Geralt, *The Last Wish*

Elves

In the fantasy realm of *The Witcher*, the elves were the first to travel from their magical realm to settle into the mainland. When humans eventually arrived and began to colonize their lands, the elves opted to take a cautious and passive approach rather than resort to immediate warfare. Over time, as a result of the humans' appetite for expansion and sense of Manifest Destiny, they began to destroy elvish settlements, assassinate their leader's heir, and systematically exterminate any that resist. The elves are eventually segregated to the nonhuman slums, along with dwarves, gnomes, halflings, and dryads. The human emperor Emhyr of Nilfgaard secretly has the infant elven prince assassinated to cut down any possibilities of succession. In a painfully similar parallel to the experiences of many marginalized cultural groups in US history, the group in power has villainized all those who stand in between them and Manifest Destiny. Early settlers were actively encouraged to tear Native Americans from their land, culture, and bodies. This was initially done through derogatory terms based on the color of their skin, paying bounties for scalped heads, and large-scale repossession of their land. Traditional native names and appreciation for the animals of the land were judged as "primitive" and used as justification for exiling them and pushing their children into boarding schools aimed at eradicating their history and way of life.

Geralt feels sympathy for the experiences of the elves, as he also identifies as an outcast. While some elves still search for nonviolent ways to avoid provoking the wrath of humans, others demand justice and self-defense through bloodshed. The Scoia'tael are a coalition of elves, dwarves, and other sympathizers who work toward raiding and killing humans they believe responsible for their people's massacre. This band of freedom fighters, sometimes known as "Squirrels," utilize guerrilla warfare tactics to wear down the human interlopers. Although it is hard to blame them for fighting back, these attacks are branded as the acts of violent revolutionaries. This is used to entrench humans further against the elves, igniting many of the explosive conflicts seen through humans and elves seen throughout *Witcher 2: Assassin of Kings*. Although the Squirrel fighters named themselves based on the appearance of their poofy looking hats, this term is also used to dehumanize them and further delegitimize their efforts. It is much easier to feel justified squirrel hunting than to admit responsibility for the genocide of a region's native population.

Sorceress

Geralt's companion and primary love interest throughout the series is an ambitious sorceress by the name of Yennefer of Vengerberg. While she was born deformed and without magical talents, she is taken in by a group of magic-users and offered an opportunity to break the glass ceiling of mediocrity she was born into. Yennefer is able to pursue her mystical studies to develop control over the chaotic elements of the world. She is granted gifts of eternal beauty and magical talents. Yennefer's spells and arcane advice are sought by some of the most powerful rulers of the land. However, nothing in life is free, and this pact requires her to sacrifice her fertility.

While this sorceress's sacrifice starts off as easy trade-off for the allure of power, charisma, and wealth that come with it, the unwritten consequences of the deal began to emerge. As sorceresses are admired for their unique abilities, they are also objectified as beautiful ornaments to be displayed around the court until needed for some more sinister purpose. At times, they are summoned by their chauvinistic masters and expected to cast a spell without question. Although given an honorary position in name only, sorceresses are seen as decorated vending machines. Without the ability to continue their lineage and create life of their own, sorceresses are bound to their oligarch's court.

Over time (and many violent international conflicts), a group of sorceresses finally gets fed up with being treated as puppets by men in charge, and they create their own coven, the Lodge of Sorceresses. However, this defection from their previous roles as indentured servants is viewed by many as threatening. The Lodge is viewed as a witch's coven, plotting from the shadows to over-throw the status quo, rather than a group of women searching for independence and self-actualization. By invalidating the Lodge's plight, sorceresses continue to be dehumanized and treated as dangerous and unpredictable.

Witchers

Although witchers were all humans at one time, the process to become a witcher can be compared to the super-soldier serum that helps create Captain America. To go through the process, only a select few with the natural constitution as well as the necessary personality traits can advance. While the process greatly enhances many of his abilities, Geralt is also left infertile, and he experiences many emotions as muted. As this process leaves witchers free from the potential for future attachments or sympathies, they are better able to stay focused on their monster-slaying creed. Unlike the deceptively charismatic nature of sorceresses, witchers are often physically deformed and reviled by others. Despite this, both witchers and sorceresses are contracted by others for their talents while treated with disgust and judgment. They are depicted as being inhuman, untrustworthy, and nothing more than a means to an end. It is because of these shared traumas Geralt and Yennefer cross paths.

In the final component of a critical quest from *Witcher 3: Wild Hunt*, Geralt faces a court of monsters that accuse him of sadistically enjoying wanton violence toward monsters. Similar to the international tribunals of war crimes held throughout history for perpetrators of violence, Geralt must present his case to a troll, a werewolf, a godling (forest prankster), and a doppler (think Mystique from X-men). The creatures interrogate him about his motives for violence and whether killing monsters is something Geralt does out of necessity or pleasure. If Geralt has shown mercy toward others and explored alternative options to always solving problems with a sword and flamethrower-like hands, he is acquitted and seen as a friend of monsters across the world. While Geralt has been the judge, jury, and executioner of many monsters in his journeys, the tables have finally turned and he is held responsible for his actions toward others. The lack of claws or a tail does not exempt someone from being a monster.

SILVER FOR MONSTERS

"Oh, Stregobor. It would be great if the cruelty of rulers could be explained away by mutations or curses."

— Geralt, The Last Wish

Traditionally, witchers wield two swords on their backs: one made of steel, meant for humans, and one made of silver, meant for monsters. While this distinction may originally seem clear-cut, Geralt frequently wrestles with how a monster is defined. The one with claws and sharp teeth? Or the one who perpetuates suffering through a calculated plan? Nonhuman creatures of the world often align with Geralt's values and show reciprocity, while humans often treat him as a pawn to accomplish their goals. Throughout the series, Geralt differentiates creatures based on their motives, whether they are acting through self-defense or a sense of honor, or whether their motives are based on manipulating others to get ahead.

Cyprian Wiley, or better known as "Whoreson Junior," is the sadistic owner of an underground empire consisting of brothels, casinos, and fighting arenas. Like many other human leaders in the Witcherverse, Whoreson primarily seeks power and kills any who stand in his way. When confronted for his brutality toward others, Geralt makes the decision to kill him and allow a doppler by the name of Dudu to transform into Whoreson and assume his leadership responsibilities. The doppler's experiences masquerading as others help him to literally walk a mile in the shoes of others, building compassion for the experiences of others. By ousting a human leader and supporting a nonhuman in taking his place, Geralt supports the ascendancy of a more humane form of government.

In response to many racial tensions emerging between humans and, well, everyone else, different radical groups begin to emerge. The Order of the White Rose is a religious cult with the explicit goal of protecting humankind from evil. Their knights templar promote the holy doctrine of the Eternal Fire, branding magic-users, elves, druids, and other creatures as a scourge on humanity. While the goal of self-preservation is enticing for many, humans quickly began to band behind the Eternal Fire based on the stoking of their fears of what they don't understand. The White Rose reinforces individuals' insecurities, that they live in a dog-eat-dog world where they will be overrun if they do not strike first. The Order's mission statement quickly transforms into extreme racism and unquestioning support for a group of crusaders and witch hunters who torture and destroy all nonhumans. Those who question and challenge the dehumanizing practices are branded as traitors.

While still generally despised, Geralt's presence is tolerated by the Order of the White Rose as a necessary evil in their campaign toward eradicating monsters. *The Witcher*'s creed has always insisted on members remaining neutral at all costs for all national matters to protect their employability status as mercenaries, regardless of where the political pendulum swings. Geralt is encouraged to align with the Order toward the destruction of various nonhuman entities, or at least stay out of their way. He's offered good coin to turn a blind eye toward the torture of various magic-users, However, Geralt refuses to be a bystander when his closest friends are persecuted for their talents as sorceresses. Akin to a magical underground railroad, Geralt helps to smuggle magic-users out of the main hub of the Order's control and fights back against dehumanization. Though his actions place a target on his back and blacklist him from many contract opportunities, Geralt breaks his monster hunter vows and forfeits payment to unite with the so-called monsters.

While many witchers prefer to keep their heads down and avoid questioning who the monster is, Geralt follows his own moral compass. Although not considered best business practice, Geralt promotes social advocacy for disenfranchised nonhumans and empathizes with the struggles that lead monsters toward self-preservation. He questions the need to kill monsters unless absolutely necessary, often finding nonviolent alternatives or scolding self-absorbed autocrats for elevating their position on the backs of others. While far from being a pacifist, Geralt's actions help to rewrite the narrative of the group in charge. He helps to understand the origin story of "the enemy" and uncover whether the monsters were truly monstrous or simply looking to live in peace.

The fantasy politics and genocide rampant in *The Witcher* show shocking parallels to the controlling actions of nonfictional leaders as well. When Germany's economy struggled in the decades following the first World War, Hitler found a platform to rise to power under his unifying vision of the Aryan race. He used fear-based propaganda to prey on the insecurities of German people, scapegoating Jewish people, the Romani, and LGBTQIA+ individuals as responsible for crippling their nation's purity and financial stability. By comparing them to "vermin" who needed to be exterminated, Hitler effectively led one of the largest dehumanization campaigns in history. The martial control of the Nazis was only possible through emphasizing differences and insisting how the survival of the two groups was incompatible. Unfortunately, Hitler was neither the first nor last tyrant to use these tactics to create cycles of hatred and dehumanization.

BREAKING THE CYCLE

"If the ability to make use of experience and draw conclusions decided, we would have forgotten what war is a long time ago. But those whose goal is war have never been held back, nor will be, by experience or analogy."

– Yennefer, *Blood of Elves*

The Knights Templar's "Holy Crusades" against Muslim people. Manifest Destiny and ousting Native Americans. Rwandan genocide. Terrorism in Gaza. Hitler's "final solution." Japanese internment camps. Abu Ghraib detention camps. Slavery, Jim Crow, and the murder of unarmed Black men by police. There are countless other historical instances of systematically dehumanizing and ignoring the meaning of a human life. Through fear-mongering and narcissism, groups of people can be rallied toward committing atrocities toward others and self-righteously hailing their actions as "for the greater good."

Without recognizing our role in it, video games have drawn the gamer into perpetuating these cycles. As long as a character is labeled as an enemy and someone else will reward me to kill them, they can be slaughtered without qualm. However, Geralt finally steps in to break this cycle by taking a moral stance toward questing. His efforts help to rehumanize the creatures who have been systematically oppressed and scapegoated for so long. Maybe this video game allegory can provide some context for our own lives and how we treat those with whom we share our environment.

The next time a quest-giver asks you to kill ten wolves, goblins, or bandits, pause before you answer. Would it change your mind if you knew your enemy's name and where they grew up? Humanity can be found in anyone, if we are willing to pause and look for it. Stop a moment and ask yourself why they need to be killed and whether there is another way that your goal can be met. Is this an extermination effort by a landowner to expand his business? Were the goblins peacefully settled away from others, cooking their dinner and raising their children? Did the so-called bandits just look to take enough to eat from the wealthy? After all, Robin Hood was nothing but a bandit in the eyes of King John.

About the Author

ALEX BAKER, PSYD is a child/adolescent clinical psychologist in the greater Boston area. He coordinates the inpatient pediatric testing services at Somerville Hospital, providing assessments focused on questions related to Autism, psychosis, and homicide risk assessments. He has worked across California, Connecticut, and Massachusetts in neuropsychological testing, residential, and outpatient treatment settings. Alex's clinical experience focuses on providing supervision, integrating testing with therapy, and providing DBT for dysregulated teenagers. He developed a group therapy curriculum based on his dissertation, helping teens to integrate everyday moral reasoning with issues of social justice. Alex is passionate about finding ways to support teens in recognizing their values and making tough ethical decisions. He uses metaphors from video games like *The Witcher* in family meetings and testing feedback sessions to help bridge intergenerational differences and reduce gamer stigma.

References

Bandura A., Underwood, B., and Fromson, M. E. (1975). "Disinhibition of aggression through diffusion of responsibility and dehumanization of victims," *Journal of Research in Personality* 9, pp. 253–269, https://doi.org/10.1016/0092-6566(75)90001-X.

Greitemeyer, T., & McLatchie, N. (2011). Denying Humanness to Others: A Newly Discovered Mechanism by Which Violent Video Games Increase Aggressive Behavior. *Psychological Science*, 22(5), 659–665. http://www.jstor.org/stable/25835431

Haidt, J. (2012). The Righteous mind: Why good people are divided by politics and religion. Pantheon/Random House.

Jiang, Z., Qi, K., Zhao, Y., Liu, J., & Lv, C. (2022). Other-Dehumanization Rather Than Self-Dehumanization Mediates the Relationship Between Violent Video Game Exposure and Aggressive Behavior. *Cyberpsychology, behavior and social networking*, 25(1), 37–42. https://doi.org/10.1089/cyber.2021.0108

Maher, Jimmy and Garriott, Richard. "*A Word on Akalabeth and Chronology*." The Digital Antiquarium. 2011-12-02. Retrieved 2023-9-17

Milgram, S. (1963). Behavioral Study of obedience. The Journal of Abnormal and Social Psychology, 67(4), 371–378. https://doi.org/10.1037/h0040525

Ntigurirwa, H. (2021). "*The Dilemma of Affirmative Rehumanization: Words Are Just the Beginning*" https://www.yalejournal.org/publications/the-dilemma-of-affirmative-rehumanization-words-are-just-the-beginning

Rediehs, L. (2014). "*From Dehumanizing to Rehumanization*," https://www.carnegiecouncil.org/media/series/ethics-online/from-dehumanization-to-rehumanization. Retrieved 2023-9-17

Wheeler, M. E., & Fiske, S. T. (2005). Controlling racial prejudice: social-cognitive goals affect amygdala and stereotype activation. *Psychological science*, *16*(1), 56–63. https://doi.org/10.1111/j.0956-7976.2005.00780.x

5

THEY ARE PEOPLE: *THE WITCHER* AND THE WOUNDED HEALER

BRYAN C. DUNCAN

"They are not demons, not devils . . .
Worse than that. They are people."

— Yennefer, *The Tower of Swallows*

C arl Jung is credited with elucidating the archetype of the wounded healer. Similarities to Greek mythology are prevalent in his work. The idea of one person giving the power of healing to another is a profound concept. This type of love and connection between humans is astounding and what binds us all together as humans. In psychology, an archetype is an inherited concept or idea that comes from human experience and is so prevalent or familiar that individuals can recognize it at an unconscious level. Some examples of archetypes are hero, wizard, sage, rebel, jester, and lover, among many others. If those roles or caricatures seem familiar, they should, not just in *The Witcher* but in innumerable stories, myths, and media. Though an oversimplification, we might shorten the concept of an archetype to psychology's version of a trope, a story, plot point, or character so often recycled and repeated they are recognized in whatever permutation almost instantly. In fact, the blending of pop culture/geekdom and psychology has produced a myriad of visual examples and charts pairing these types of roles to characters from almost any fandom imaginable.

The wounded healer is known to the psychology field and is present in the world at large. This scenario is marked best when a person is compelled to help another person due, at least in part, to their own psychological wounds. In turn, these wounds provide the compassion to heal others. Self-examination provides healing for the the healer while they are helping to heal another. For some, the driving factor to heal others is their own psychological wounds. Sometimes they choose this path to help or rescue others who are facing similar concerns. Perhaps they choose to be a healer to better understand their own wounds and how to heal themselves, finding tools to share with others on the way. Finally, they may want to understand those that hurt them, hoping to prevent or break the cycle of harm passed from one person to another. Additionally, any combination of the above motives may drive a person to becoming a wounded healer. Though any witcher from the series would make a great example of a wounded healer, for specific purposes, Geralt of Rivia himself is an excellent focus, due to his central role across the books, games, and television series.

Geralt has many wounds to choose from, as they are what drives him in his protection and empathy for others: being abandoned to the witchers by his mother, the loss of friends and comrades during training, betrayal by other witcher groups and a king, and the trauma that continues throughout his career. While not a healer in the traditional sense of physician or medicine, Geralt finds himself healing communities that are suffering from the presence of the evil he fights. Villagers, leaders, and NPCs, in terms of the games, seek Geralt's help and support in dealing with the problems in their communities, families, or other situations. Geralt helps them through vanquishing the evil and clears the way for healing and recovery. Therefore, despite him not being an apothecary or provider of physical medical support, Geralt is a healer, setting wrongs to right, overcoming pervasive evils, and removing barriers to community recovery.

A PITIFUL DEFENSE
AGAINST BEING DIFFERENT

"I manage because I have to . . . Because I've overcome the vanity and pride of being different. I've understood that they are a pitiful defense against being different."

— Geralt, *The Last Wish*

Summarizing the entire saga of *The Witcher* in a brief paragraph is impossible, as it contains at least eight books, three video games, eight other games, a couple of adaptations to film, and a television series. Instead, it is best to just skip straight to the point: Geralt, trauma, empathy, and protection. In the lore, Geralt is exposed to mutagens in his youth that have profound impact on his physiology, isolating him from the humans around him. The books contain stories of soldiers killing Geralt's fellow witchers. Bandits have attempted to kill him, kings and communities have banned him, and he has suffered many other indignities and injuries at the hands of humans and monsters alike. Continually, Geralt fights monsters, saves humans, and seems compelled to do so regardless of the suspicion and trauma he has faced. An entire chapter of this book could be devoted to debating whether Geralt does these things despite his traumas and losses, as he has emotionally poignant moments in which he thinks of giving up the life of a witcher in the lore, or because of his pain and wounds he has an overwhelming empathy for the hurts of others, as he seeks to protect others from the sufferings he has endured himself. The question of why Geralt does what he does is for another discussion; what remains is the witcher as a flawed rescuer, a wounded healer.

Throughout the *Witcher* franchise, Geralt of Rivia is driven to face dark and dangerous entities with dark and dangerous aspects within himself. Geralt's experiences give him insight into how to fight creatures afflicting a village. As such there are times that the experience and intimate knowledge of the enemy is then met with relief and comfort by the people Geralt encounters. Similarly, there are times that therapists are valued and sought due to their own personal encounters with the condition in question. When looking for a healer, sometimes those who need healing feel most comfortable with someone who has had personal experiences with trauma. This gives them the idea that somehow this person may understand them better than those who have not experienced trauma in a similar capacity. There is some evidence that those seeking help find others who match them demographically. For example, there is some evidence that at least some people find more solace confiding in someone the same gender as themselves. This is even present in such details as racial and ethnic background. Sometimes, this is the bridge to success for the healer and the person they are attempting to heal. Though gender and race do not in and of themselves indicate an exact match in life experiences, it could be assumed that those who seek such similarities are looking for someone that understands the context of their life. Just as those who seek Geralt's help may ask, "Have you ever faced . . . ?" seeking the validation that such troubles are not uniquely their own. This intimate understanding of what someone is facing, what is at stake, and what must be done to overcome it, is a draw for them to seek the wounded healer.

 COMPASSION, SYMPATHY, AND DEDICATION

"If someone shows you compassion, sympathy and dedication, if they surprise you with integrity of character, value it but don't mistake it for . . . something else."

– Yarpen Zigrin, *Blood of Elves*

Geralt often finds himself struggling with his identity. This is powerfully evident in the streaming series, when he at some times identifies as a mutant, and at others, admitting his flaws and failings, is powerfully human. Geralt can be seen to fight the darkness in himself: his eyes change, and dark blood courses through his veins. Both ironic and iconic, this internal struggle is most apparent when his struggles against external evils are most intense. Geralt as the wounded healer faces a similar internal struggle. Despite his modifications and powers, Geralt is human and scarred, just as healers are wounded people too, who face the same struggles and concerns as others. The healer's own experiences, symptoms, and diagnoses may give them a profound perspective on the issues their friends or acquaintances are facing. On the other hand, the unexpected confrontation with a reflection of their own pain can be activating, distressing, or even retraumatizing for the therapist.

Geralt's struggles with evil give him a unique insight into facing the darkness ahead. He sees that reflection of pain and struggle in the characters around him, such as Yennefer and Ciri. At times, he faces similar enemies and is confronted with reminders of old conflicts and hurts. This is a cycle Geralt faces at each conflict, as new wounds are incurred on top of old ones. In this, we can see how the healer can sometimes experience activating stimuli when helping someone. This can be overwhelming and retraumatizing to the healer, as the painful events that once occurred in the healer's life are now brought to the surface because of someone else's pain. Facing vicarious trauma or re-traumatization, healers may find themselves struggling with what role their own wounds are playing in their attempts at working with others. It is important that emotions that arise for healers are also given adequate time to be processed. When their own wounds are interfering with their ability to work with others, it is time to take a step back. Geralt does not get this break, typically, and in the books he considers walking away from the witcher life several times, indicating burnout.

Traditionally, struggling helpers would be encouraged to seek their own support or, "do your own work." In some therapeutic approaches, for example, the practice of therapists having their own therapist is still very much encouraged. In the broader sense of the mental health field, they are often advised to be mindful of their own self-care. This is a practice that is helpful and necessary for everyone in the world. Sometimes, a healer can give so much to someone else that they lose themselves and their needs in the process. This vaguer notion of caring for the self can more often be heard as encouragement between mental health workers than the specific advice to seek therapy. Therapy can be beneficial to everyone to discover more about themselves and be in a better space to help others. Geralt himself seeks the support of his allies at several points in the narrative, illustrating that though he may usually work alone, he also recognizes limits and seeks support.

Geralt, unfortunately, faces judgment and distrust from those who are suspicious of witchers. While not explicitly stated, Geralt's tendency to work alone may be an attempt to protect others from derision, and the guilt over placing those he cares for at risk. Similarly, the real world's stigma around psychological struggles can be both socially imposed and self-imposed. Some individuals may experience guilt or shame when reaching out for help, fearing judgment. Perhaps they are the type of person who seems to "have it all together." Seeking therapy for themselves might make them feel that they cannot keep up this appearance, on which they place so much importance. Instead, the healer may choose to remain silent, and they risk reaching a point where it is difficult to access empathy for others. This fight for self-control may lead a person to feel their emotions are barely contained, just as Geralt seems to barely contain the forces within him at the pinnacle of his struggles.

In the novels, Geralt considers leaving the witchers as he grapples with the burdens such a perilous path brings. He talks about his internal struggle and ultimately chooses to continue to walk the path of a witcher. In the real world, the culture of stigma and the wounded healers' silence, and the complex and difficult emotions that may arise during the process (for both healer and wounded), may worsen the issues. Such struggles can also impede the recovery of the healer, which could result in their attempt at helping someone else being ineffective. In short, the healer may burn out. And the results can be disastrous.

An internal struggle may occur as someone continues to gain insight into their own wounds while containing and processing difficult situations and experiences in others. They may therefore face complex and difficult emotions in the healing process, their own and those of others, both as healer and wounded.

THEY SEEM LESS MONSTROUS

"People . . . like to invent monsters and monstrosities.
Then they seem less monstrous themselves."

– Geralt, *The Last Wish*

This conflicted sense of hero and troubled or dangerous individual plays out in the responses Geralt receives from the people he helps. He is jeered or lauded, at times one and then the other by the same group of people. Revealing yourself as a healer, particularly a wounded one, can come with similar risks. As an example, borderline personality disorder carries a stigma among some individuals and groups. Often, those diagnosed with borderline personality disorder may feel unable to disclose to others in fear of this stigma. This stigma could be birthed from a perception, albeit antiquated, that the condition is untreatable. Or it may arise from the lack of understanding of this condition. It is reasonable to assume that any condition that is poorly understood in the general population—which is arguably most conditions—could be perceived as an untreatable or a permanent condition and state. Geralt may seem dangerous and irredeemable to the villagers and others, particularly as they do not understand him or his role as a witcher.

Perhaps those who reject Geralt perceive him as infected with evil, as if interaction with him presents a risk of the spread of evil. In a real-world example, COVID-19 presented a whole new set of challenges for helpers. Discrimination is prevalent in some regarding the mental health consequences connected with COVID-19. The highest instances of discrimination seemed to be in reference to depression, particularly if the severity was high enough that the individual was reporting high levels of distress. This risk or perceived risk may discourage wounded healers, not only from disclosing but also from seeking their own treatment. While depression was at the forefront of this stigma, it is reasonable to generalize this feeling of being stigmatized to other conditions, particularly those accompanied by psychological distress, which, again, is arguably most mental health conditions.

The mistrust of those around him could also discourage Geralt from seeking support from the villagers or keep both the villagers and Geralt from allowing for a way to mobilize the populous themselves against the evil. Instead, Geralt often faces dangers alone. Much like Geralt, it is understandable that the wounded healer would consider leaving the profession, finding a trade that is less painful and more peaceful.

KNOW ABOUT SOMETHING, IT STOPS BEING A NIGHTMARE

"When you know about something, it stops being a nightmare. When you know how to fight something, it stops being so threatening."

– Uncle Vesemir, *Blood of Elves*

So many healers face their own wounds. After all, no one lives a life free of suffering. The obvious question arises: does having a wound make the helper a better healer? The argument can be made for Geralt, who knows how to respond and recover from the circumstances he finds himself in because he has seen much of it before; his experiences improve his abilities. It is possible that being wounded may improve the work of the healer, perhaps by increasing empathy, but such a conclusion remains unproven, though fields like peer support and substance abuse recovery have utilized the concept of "one who has walked this path" almost from their beginning.

The reverse is just as likely, that unchecked and untreated wounds may lead the healer to do the very things that produce feelings of shame, not just in the individual but to all who heal. This in turn may increase the stigma some carry for the wounded healer. This also perpetuates the cycle of "hurt people hurt people." Individuals hurt in sexual ways may risk reenacting that trauma, feeling a sexual attraction for the person they intend to help, and left unchecked, this may result in inappropriate or predatory sexual relationships as the healer manipulates and abuses the power in the relationship and takes advantage of the one they originally intended to help. It may be the tendency of the helper to not talk, due to the aforementioned stigmas, about being wounded and their own personal struggles that exacerbate these dangers.

Instead, an open and more transparent discussion with another healer or mentor may prevent the wounded healer from inadvertently causing harm to one they intend to help. The model for such dialogue should begin in the training and mentorship of aspiring healers—more on that in a moment. Openness and support may foster growth and resilience in those who are wounded and intend to help others. Geralt asserts that he fights monsters, not humans, to the magician Stregobor and is met with the counter that humans may in some cases be the worse monster. Unfortunately, throughout the books and series, Geralt finds himself hurting others even when that is not his goal.

As Geralt travels, fights, and adventures, he incurs wounds. Not only is he wounded to start, but he is also further wounded by the actual practice of being a witcher. The practice of healing is no different. A healer may not only be wounded as they start in their chosen profession, but they may be further wounded by the ongoing practice of the healing. Vicarious trauma is the process by which the healer is horrified or otherwise severely psychologically disturbed by the trauma the hurt individual shares. This is particularly a risk as those who are hurting reveal extreme traumas again and again to the healer. There are also issues like individuals becoming obsessed, stalking, or potentially assaulting someone who is helping them. Obviously, such events would not only result in physical and psychological wounds to those attempting to help; they would also create some complex emotions around the process of helping.

It may be difficult for that healer to continue to heal. They may cease to help others due to the trauma. Healers sometimes experience higher risks of anxiety and depression due to coping with their own wounds and those of others. Grief and loss is present for the healer, should they lose someone they are trying to help, whether to suicide or natural causes. The loss of someone a healer is trying to help through death is unpredictable. Geralt faces grief and loss in his adventures, and at times it seems these wounds are often his most grievous. It is loss and grief that threatens to push him from his work the most.

 NEVER BLAME OTHERS FOR THEM

"Mistakes . . . are also important to me. I don't cross them out of my life, or memory. And I never blame others for them."

– Geralt, *Blood of Elves*

Healers are frequently involved in the creation of other healers. As the story of Geralt unfolds, he meets Ciri and trains her as the next generation of witcher. While Ciri's traumas are not the focus of this chapter, with the loss of her family, kingdom, home etc., it is fair to say she also carries wounds. Part of training Ciri to be a witcher involves Geralt teaching her to manage and contain her pain and wounds. As all people carry the wounds and scars of their experiences, helping future healers to address their wounds and manage their pain to be more effective healers is essential. Those who train other healers have a responsibility not only to their trainee but also to the society at large to help the trainee identify and find healthy ways to address their wounds. This process of addressing the wound and tending to wellness protects the public by reducing the chances of the "hurt people hurt people" discussed above. This process of trainers identifying wounds that need to be addressed and risks in the work for the healer is an essential practice. Though different approaches might be taken to looking for wounds that may impair the future healer depending on the type or degree of training, it is always present.

Dealing with negative experiences and promoting wellness and care does not stop at personal situations and difficulties, but also into things like conflicts with others and even negative reactions to those who train healers. Tackling such issues is a core skill of a healer and therefore critical to learn. Handling aggression, taking a hit, and being able to remain resilient even in the most challenging of situations are all skills a warrior like Geralt would pass to Ciri. He essentially teaches her not to let her wounds and pain get the better of her, but scars provide important lessons in facing the harsh realities of being a witcher.

How then do wounded healers deal with their pain? How does a conscientious healer keep their own struggles from impacting their work? It is important to be open and honest about their struggles. Find a co-healer or mentor to help identify risky issues and offer solutions to resolving them. Part of that resolution will likely involve doing their own work with their own healer. This may require them to overcome stigma and discrimination. Though the way of a healer is hard, and they may consider giving it up in much the same way Geralt considers leaving the witchers, it remains a worthwhile pursuit. Often the struggles of being human are what drive someone to be a healer to begin with, to help and support others. Just as a major theme of *The Witcher* franchise is Geralt dealing with his own struggles, part of being an effective healer is dealing with your own wounds. Geralt must face his issues for the betterment of himself, and deals with the tragedies for the good of those he protects; so too must the healer. Geralt also passes on what he has learned and how to deal with pain and trauma just as much as the monsters; so too a healing mentor trains a healer not only in their practice but also in what to do with their own hurt. Geralt sets an example for Ciri, just as the wounded healer sets a model of how to handle the wound for the next generation of healers. After all, everyone has wounds. What is most important is how those are handled when helping others. "The point is how it is borne."

About the Author

DR. BRYAN C. DUNCAN is a Licensed Psychologist, Licensed Professional Counselor, Supervisor and Nationally Certified Counselor, the Director of Clinical and Training Services at New Leaf Services and Assistant Training Director of Psychology at John Peter Smith Hospital in Fort Worth, Texas. He is a Certified Geek Therapist, a Certified Therapeutic Game Master, and Certified Problematic Gaming Specialist from Geek Therapeutics. Among his areas of expertise are: cognitive behavioral therapy (CBT), Acceptance and Commitment Therapy (ACT), Dialectical Behavior Therapy (DBT) and cognitive processing therapy (CPT), Prolonged Exposure Therapy (PE), and Trauma Focused CBT (TF-CBT), therapy for traumatic experiences, abuse, post-traumatic stress disorder (PTSD), grief counseling, and health issues (including therapy for adjusting to chronic medical conditions; sleep difficulties; exercise, diet, and medical treatment adherence).

References

Cabral, R. R., & Smith, T. B. (2011). Racial/ethnic matching of clients and therapists in mental health services: a meta-analytic review of preferences, perceptions, and outcomes. *Journal of Counseling Psychology, 58*(4), 537–554. https://doi.org/10.1037/a0025266

Conchar, C., & Repper, J. (2014), ""Walking wounded or wounded healer?" Does personal experience of mental health problems help or hinder mental health practice? A review of the literature." *Mental Health and Social Inclusion, 18*(1). 35–44. https://doi.org/10.1108/MHSI-02–2014–0003

Farber, S. K. (2016). *Celebrating the Wounded Healer Psychotherapist: Pain, Post-Traumatic Growth and Self Disclosure.* Routledge.

Jung, C. G. (1966). *The Practice of Psychotherapy 2ⁿᵈ Edition.* Princeton University Press

Mediavilla, R., Fernández-Jiménez, E., Andreo, J., Morán-Sánchez, I., Muñoz-Sanjosé, A.,

Moreno-Küstner, B., Mascayano, F., Ayuso-Mateos, J. L., Bravo-Ortiz, M. F., Martínez-Alés, G., & COVID 19 HEalth caRe wOrkErS Spain HEROESSPA Working Group (2021). Association between perceived discrimination and mental health outcomes among health workers during the initial COVID-19 outbreak. Revista de psiquiatria y salud mental, S1888–9891(21)00062–8. Advance online publication. https://doi.org/10.1016/j.rpsm.2021.06.001

O'Brien, J. M., (2011). Wounded healer: Psychotherapist grief over a client's death. *Professional Psychology: Research and Practice*, *42*(3), 236–243. https://doi.org/10.1037/a0023788

Pikus, C.F., & Heavey, C.L. (1996). Client preferences for therapist gender. *Journal of College Student Psychotherapy*, *10*, 35–43.

Ring, D., & Lawn, S. (2019) Stigma perpetuation at the interface of mental health care: a review to compare patient and clinician perspectives of stigma and borderline personality disorder, *Journal of Mental Health*, DOI: 10.1080/09638237.2019.1581337

Wheeler, S. (2007). What shall we do with the wounded healer? The supervisor's dilemma. *Psychodynamic Practice*, *13*(3), 245–256, doi:10.1080/144753630701455838

Zerubavel, N., & Wright, M. O. (2012). The dilemma of the wounded healer. *Psychotherapy*, *49*(4), 482–491. https://doi.org/10.1037/a0027824

6

THE WHITE WOLF'S GRAY HAIRS: ETHICS ARE NOT BLACK AND WHITE

LOU ANNA CLAVEAU

"Evil is evil. Lesser, greater, middling, makes no difference. The degree is arbitrary, the definitions blurred. If I'm to choose between one evil and another, I'd rather not choose at all."

— *The Witcher 3: Wild Hunt*

This exploration delves into Geralt of Rivia's moral decision-making, scrutinizing its impact on relationships within *The Witcher*'s diverse world. As a complex character, Geralt's charismatic yet brutal nature draws attention and defense, especially in light of the actor's portrayal. This analysis extends beyond the character's surface, exploring the extensive RPG character development and the immersive experience it offers. Drawing on theories from Kohlberg and Piaget, we examine the interplay between Geralt's thought and action, shedding light on moral development and its link to adaptation or withdrawal within *The Witcher*'s narrative.

One important exploration focus is Geralt's upbringing in an isolated environment dominated by male role models. We will scrutinize the absence of maternal influence in relation to his ideals, mores, and moral development, raising questions about the impact of his "gray" morality. Geralt's unique origin as a witcher, shaped by the forced consumption of a concoction, results in a superhuman with distinct ideals that clash with the world. Despite facing adversity, Geralt's sought-after presence is evident, drawing attention to the popularity and defense of the character, notably portrayed by Henry Cavill in the first two seasons of the Netflix show, and thereafter by Liam Hemsworth. This popularity is linked to Geralt's nonjudgmental, morally gray nature and his famous line, "The world doesn't need a hero; it needs a professional."

Our focus then shifts to the framework of geek therapy, gaming, and self-concept about morals, referencing Piaget's stages of moral development. Contemplation is given to how Geralt's sense of justice evolves in the gaming world, drawing parallels to real-world grief within the context of fantasy gaming. We conclude by addressing the real-world impact of Henry Cavill's departure from *The Witcher*, noting widespread anger and a desire to rectify a perceived wrong. The dynamic between defending a fictional character and a real-life actor prompts ethical and moral questioning. Despite varied fan perceptions based on the initial portrayal, the exploration suggests that, as depicted in the series, the game, and the author's words, Geralt remains firmly in the realm of moral ambiguity. Kohlberg's dilemmas for determining moral development stages are presented below, accompanied by a chart detailing the stages and potential outcomes.

Kohlberg's Theory is a six-stage concept arranged with varying and successive levels of complexity showing evolving growth due to maturity, age, and experience.

Level 1: Preconventional level

At this level, we see Piaget's influence as morals are controlled externally. Conforming means avoidance of punishment. There is more at stake here than personal gratification. There are two sublevels to this stage.

Stage 1: Punishment/obedience orientation

Compliance means lack of or avoidance of consequences to the negative behavior.

Stage 2: Instrumental purpose orientation

The consequences of compliance mean reward rather than punishment.

Level 2: Conventional level

Here, social rules are essential, and there is a shift from self to others, which includes relationships with others and regulations set forth by social systems, including the government, family, and school environment, to name a few. The idea here is that supporting these rules provides a societal operational framework.

Stage 3: Good/Nice orientation

Put: How others view me. Am I a "good" person or a "nice" person? Where do I lie on the moral stage?

Stage 4: Law and order orientation

Governmentally structured rules and laws will determine the need for behavior and social acceptance. This view means the individual has come to accept and learn the world outside of self, and small social groups—family, for instance—take on more meaning. There is a belief that these are worth maintaining and teaching to future generations.

Level 3: Postconventional or principled level

This level ends Piaget's influence, as he did not expound any further. Kohlberg, however, splits this level into two additional sublevels. This becomes an abstraction of social norms, mores, and morals. This is morals applied to all situations and purposes. Kohlberg begins the idea of gray morality.

Stage 5: Social contract orientation

Individual rights determine behavior. This is the rule that proves the exception. There are alternatives to be considered. Rules are flexible and open to improving human purposes.

Stage 6: Universal ethical principle orientation

According to Kohlberg, this is the highest stage of functioning and one that few, if any, of us ever attain. This ethical and moral development examines individuals and society to determine "right" and "wrong." Something that Geralt is very good at doing.

 PROFESSIONALISM AND UNIVERSAL ETHICS

Geralt's line, "This world doesn't need a hero; it needs a professional," encapsulates the essence of his professional approach to being a witcher. This professional demeanor, characterized by adherence to specific guidelines, duty-bound responsibilities, and a commitment to professionalism, significantly contributes to the gray morality that defines Geralt's character.

Beyond the confines of the traditional hero archetype, Geralt's professionalism reflects a nuanced understanding of the moral complexities inherent in the world. Unlike conventional heroes who might operate within clear-cut distinctions of good and evil, Geralt navigates a morally ambiguous landscape. His decisions and actions are guided by a universal sense of ethics, demonstrating a commitment to a higher standard that transcends simplistic moral binaries.

Geralt's professional ethos is crucial in his role as a morally gray character. Instead of succumbing to rigid notions of right and wrong, he operates within a framework that acknowledges the shades of gray within the moral spectrum. This approach is particularly evident in his interactions with various characters and situations, where he is confronted with choices that don't neatly fit into conventional moral categories.

The emphasis on professionalism and universal ethics in Geralt's character adds depth to his moral stance. It underscores his capacity to make decisions that align with a broader understanding of morality—one that considers the intricacies and nuances of each situation. This approach allows Geralt to navigate the complexities of a world rife with moral ambiguity, where straightforward distinctions between good and evil often blur.

In practical terms, Geralt's professionalism manifests in his ability to make decisions based on carefully assessing the circumstances and weighing the potential consequences and ethical implications. This pragmatic and measured approach sets him apart from characters who might adhere strictly to a black and white moral framework. It also positions him as a character who strives to uphold a set of principles that transcend the immediate context of each decision while operating in a morally gray space.

Ultimately, Geralt's commitment to professionalism and universal ethics contributes to the rich moral tapestry of the *Witcher* series. His character serves as a lens through which players can explore the complexities of morality in a world marked by shades of gray. By embodying a professional ethos that transcends simplistic moral distinctions, Geralt becomes a compelling and multifaceted protagonist, challenging players to engage with the moral intricacies of the narrative in a thoughtful and nuanced manner.

MORAL DILEMMAS IN GAMEPLAY

The Witcher franchise, known for its intricate narrative and morally gray characters, continually engages players with challenging moral dilemmas that mirror the complexities of Geralt's own decisions. Players confront situations that force them to make difficult choices throughout the game, often involving the delicate balance between individual lives and broader moral principles.

One standout example that encapsulates the nuanced moral landscape of *The Witcher* is the quest involving the Bloody Baron, in *The Witcher 3: Wild Hunt*. This character, marked by moral ambiguity and a history of heinous acts, becomes a focal point for players to grapple with questions of redemption, forgiveness, and the consequences of their actions. The quest places players in the position of deciding whether to aid the Baron in his quest for redemption or allow him to face the total weight of accountability for his past deeds.

The Bloody Baron quest emulates the intricate moral tapestry woven into the game's narrative. Players are not presented with clear-cut choices between good and evil but are instead forced to navigate moral ambiguity and nuance. The quest challenges players to consider the Baron's potential for redemption, weighing it against the severity of his crimes and the broader moral principles at play.

This moral dilemma is a microcosm of Geralt's struggles with morality throughout the series. As a morally gray character, Geralt often finds himself in situations where the boundaries between right and wrong are less distinct. The quest involving the Bloody Baron mirrors Geralt's constant navigation of moral complexities, reinforcing the theme that decisions in *The Witcher* universe are rarely straightforward.

The beauty of these moral dilemmas lies in their capacity to engage players on a deeper level, prompting them to reflect on their ethical values and principles. By presenting choices that require consideration of both individual circumstances and broader moral implications, the game encourages players to think beyond simplistic moral binaries.

Moreover, the consequences of these choices resonate throughout the game, shaping the narrative and influencing the relationships Geralt forms with other characters. This interconnected web of consequences reinforces the notion that morality in *The Witcher* is not a static concept but a fluid and evolving one shaped by the decisions made by both players and Geralt.

The quest involving the Bloody Baron is a testament to *The Witcher*'s commitment to portraying moral ambiguity. By forcing players to confront the complexities of redemption, forgiveness, and accountability, the game offers an immersive experience beyond conventional notions of morality. It becomes a journey into the heart of ethical decision-making, mirroring the intricate moral struggles of Geralt himself.

GERALT'S MORAL CODE

Geralt of Rivia is known for his distinctive moral code, which often falls along a morally gray spectrum. This is evident in his approach to killing monsters. While his mantra suggests a clear-cut distinction between "Monster = Bad" and "Human = Good," Geralt's actions reflect a more nuanced perspective. He doesn't mindlessly slay creatures but instead evaluates the circumstances and provides warnings, showcasing a more complex view of morality. In addition to this complex decision-making, he sometimes needs more time to study the situation before acting. In these cases, Geralt's demeanor and facial expressions say it all, with a pained grimace that says "Why?!" His decisions are not solely based on rigid rules; instead, Geralt considers the context, motivations, and potential consequences. This fluidity in his moral compass is a crucial aspect of his character that resonates with audiences. Unlike traditional heroes with unwavering ideals, Geralt navigates a world filled with shades of gray.

Geralt is sent to *The Witchers* at the School of the Wolf. There, his sense of right and wrong develops through studies of violence and monsters, and he adopts a straightforward mantra: Monster bad, human good. Kill monster, save human. Initially, humans are deemed worth saving and preserving, while monsters are condemned. However, as Geralt matures and gains experience in the real world, beyond the protective walls of his school, his perspective evolves.

Not much is revealed about his time before the collapse and attack on Kaer Morhen, his beloved home. Being raised with a set of principles that define good and evil is a societal standard. How that definition changes depends on environmental factors, maturity, and life experiences.

THE BUTCHER OF BLAVIKEN

Geralt's infamous title, the "Butcher of Blaviken," stems from a moment in his past that epitomizes the moral ambiguity surrounding his actions. Faced with a difficult choice in Blaviken, Geralt reluctantly kills a woman who chooses him as the instrument of her death. This event haunts him, illustrating the consequences of adhering to a strict moral code in a complex world. She has sent three adversaries against him, which he dispatches. This is the first of his "Why?!" face that we see.

The Butcher of Blaviken incident underscores the theme that sometimes, doing the right thing can still lead to negative consequences. It becomes a defining moment in Geralt's life, shaping his understanding of morality and reinforcing the moral ambiguity of his choices.

In the encounter with the kikimora, Geralt is depicted as ingesting a potion to aid in the impending battle, introducing two socially unacceptable elements: violence and drug-induced enhancement. However, Geralt's actions reveal a controlled and calculated approach to dealing with threats to the greater good. The kikimora is dispatched, and in a surprising turn, Geralt notices a helpless fawn near a pond. Despite the harsh context of the situation, Geralt's response is marked by a heavy heart as he remarks, "It just isn't your day, is it?"

Notably, the narrative choice to withhold the graphic details of the killing and cooking of the fawn raises questions about the potential avoidance of moral outrage. This decision showcases a deliberate narrative strategy, allowing players and viewers to focus on the broader moral implications of Geralt's actions rather than dwelling on graphic violence. The narrative further explores Geralt's involvement in the fate of Jaskier (Dandelion), a recurring character often needing rescue. Despite Jaskier's bumbling and questionable choices, Geralt consistently becomes the moral compass by which both men are judged. Geralt's repeated interventions for Jaskier highlight his adherence to the foundational principle instilled in him: "Monster bad, human good." This unwavering commitment to his moral code is central to Geralt's character, demonstrating his consistency even in chaotic and unpredictable situations.

As the narrative progresses, Geralt's role as Ciri's father figure adds another layer of moral complexity. Claiming the Law of Surprise when saving Ciri's father and, consequently, her mother, Geralt becomes bound to accept the consequences of this decision. The subsequent upbringing of Ciri involves imparting that foundational principle while sheltering her from the harsh rites of becoming a full-fledged witcher. This decision unveils the cruelty of the transformative ritual, highlighting Geralt's moral stance against subjecting Ciri to the same fate as other witchers.

The introduction of Yennefer and Triss Marigold into Ciri's life to address her feminine needs goes beyond mere practicality. In fulfilling their roles, these women provide a more profound purpose by offering love, patience, understanding, and a moral compass that contrasts with the harsh standards prevalent among the male witchers. Geralt's acceptance of this unconventional approach underscores his adaptability and desire to ensure Ciri's well-rounded upbringing, transcending the traditional boundaries of his profession.

The narrative also delves into the dynamics between Geralt and Vesemir, the latter serving as a mentor and father figure. Despite Vesemir's initial resistance to acknowledging the care he receives from Geralt, the narrative suggests a level of familial connection that goes beyond the typical mentor-student relationship. This dynamic showcases Geralt's sense of responsibility and care for those he considers part of his extended family. As the school's oldest "active" witcher, Geralt's guidance extends not only to younger witchers but also to Vesemir in a filial role.

While Vesemir may initially reject this notion, the narrative implies a gradual acceptance, illustrating a level of care that allows personal freedom within their relationship. This portrayal of familial bonds adds a nuanced layer to Geralt's character, emphasizing his capacity for emotional connections amid the harshness of his world.

In essence, Geralt's narrative arc in the world of *The Witcher* is a crucial exploration of his moral stance and decision-making. Consistent adherence to his principles and nuanced approaches to complex situations cements Geralt as a complex and balanced character. The narrative invites players and viewers to reflect on morality, duty, and the consequences of choices in a world that often defies simplistic categorizations of good and evil.

 ALL GROWN UP?

Moving on to a more adult Geralt, he learns about how governments function, his role in the world, and the skills required to survive as a witcher. Beyond the gates of Kaer Morhen, he discovers that more people harbor hatred than welcome him; even those who welcome him do so with caution and fear, often with disdain.

During Geralt's journey, the narrative takes a closer look at his understanding of the broader world outside the confines of Kaer Morhen. This phase of his development involves a deep dive into the intricacies of governance, Geralt's role within the societal framework, and honing skills crucial for survival as a witcher. Geralt's initiation into the functioning of governments provides a lens through which he perceives the larger socio-political landscape. This knowledge becomes pivotal in shaping his interactions with various factions, rulers, and power structures. Understanding the political dynamics adds another layer of complexity to Geralt's character, highlighting his awareness of the intricate balance between individual agency and systemic influences.

The revelation that more people harbor hatred than extend open arms sets the stage for his challenges. The caution and fear with which he is met, even by those who ostensibly welcome him, use him, and define his role within their schemes, underline the pervasive prejudice and mistrust directed toward witchers. This theme of societal apprehension serves as a recurring motif, emphasizing the dichotomy between Geralt's essential role as a protector and the societal disdain he faces. It suggests that, despite the surface-level acceptance, prejudice and unease remain as undercurrents. This nuanced portrayal adds depth to the narrative, painting a world where individuals are torn between recognizing the necessity of a witcher's skills and succumbing to ingrained societal biases. This is something often faced by those who choose violence to preserve peace.

Geralt's experiences contribute to the shaping of his character and moral outlook. The dichotomy of being both needed and resented by the society he strives to protect forms a crucial aspect of his moral dilemmas. This phase lays the foundation for the intricate web of relationships and conflicts that characterize Geralt's interactions in the subsequent levels of his narrative arc.

This is a pivotal stage in Geralt's growth, exposing him to the complexities of political structures, societal biases, and the challenges inherent in being a witcher. The narrative deftly weaves these elements into the fabric of Geralt's character, setting the stage for the moral quandaries and decisions that will define his journey in *The Witcher*'s world.

Geralt has accumulated centuries of knowledge, wisdom, and experience with man and beast. Blending dedication, respect for his mentor Vesemir, unwavering dedication to his profession and brothers, and a set of values, Geralt emerges as a morally gray and balanced character throughout the franchise. Geralt's approach to killing is clarified; he doesn't randomly kill but instead hunts monsters, while humans seem to seek him out. He provides warnings and reasons for engaging or not engaging in battle with monsters or individuals. The narrative explores Geralt's actions in specific situations, such as his encounter with the kikimora and injured fawn.

The narrative propels Geralt into the world of *The Witcher*, a realm where his accumulated centuries of knowledge, wisdom, and experience become the defining elements of his character. This phase marks a crucial juncture in Geralt's evolution, showcasing a synthesis of dedication, respect, and a steadfast commitment to his profession and the Brotherhood of witchers and, as a result, the need to navigate the intricate web of moral dilemmas.

Central to Geralt's moral compass is his refined approach to killing. The narrative explicitly clarifies that he doesn't engage in random acts of violence but instead focuses on hunting monsters, a task for which he is sought by both man and beast. This deliberate choice to specialize in hunting monsters distinguishes Geralt's moral stance, aligning with his foundational principle.

FORGIVENESS AND REDEMPTION: A LINK FOR THE LEAP FROM CONCRETE TO UNIVERSAL ETHICS

The Witcher's recurrent theme of forgiveness and redemption challenges players to grapple with the possibilities of transformation in a world characterized by moral ambiguity. Geralt's interactions with characters such as the Bloody Baron and others who are morally flawed serve as pivotal moments that invite players to contemplate the intricacies of redemption. Geralt's capacity to engage with characters who have committed grave mistakes reflects a nuanced perspective on morality—one that acknowledges the potential for individuals to change and seeks avenues for forgiveness. The narrative deliberately introduces morally complex figures, providing players with opportunities to explore the boundaries of redemption in a world where moral lines are often blurred.

The exploration of forgiveness and redemption becomes a central aspect of *The Witcher*'s moral tapestry. Geralt's encounters with characters marked by their past misdeeds underscore *The Witcher*'s commitment to presenting a world where individuals, no matter how morally compromised, are not entirely condemned to a fixed fate. This theme resonates with players as they navigate the intricate moral landscape, prompting them to confront questions about the malleability of morality and the possibility of redemption in a world fraught with moral dilemmas.

The character of the Bloody Baron serves as a poignant illustration of this theme. Through Geralt's interactions with the Baron, players are presented with a character burdened by grave mistakes and moral failings. The narrative unfolds in a way that challenges players to consider whether redemption is achievable for someone who has committed such heinous acts. The emotional depth of these encounters contributes to a narrative that transcends mere binary notions of good and evil, encouraging players to reflect on the complex interplay between actions, consequences, and the potential for personal transformation.

Through its exploration of forgiveness and redemption, the *Witcher* series demonstrates a commitment to portraying a morally nuanced world where characters grapple with the consequences of their choices. The theme becomes a powerful tool for prompting players to engage in introspection, challenging preconceptions about the irreversibility of moral transgressions, and inviting them to consider the potential for redemption, even in the face of seemingly insurmountable darkness.

In essence, *The Witcher* weaves a narrative that delves into the intricate terrain of forgiveness and redemption, leaving players with a profound exploration of the possibilities for change and transformation in a morally complex and ambiguous world. Through Geralt's journey, the franchise invites viewers, readers, and players to confront their beliefs about morality and redemption, fostering a thoughtful and reflective experience.

UNIVERSAL ACCEPTANCE OF FATE

Moreover, Geralt's interactions with monsters and humans unveil a nuanced perspective. Rather than succumbing to a black and white worldview, he provides warnings and reasons for his decisions in battles, emphasizing a calculated and measured approach. This willingness to engage in discourse and offer alternatives reflects Geralt's commitment to justice and a rejection of blind violence, as seen in the encounter with the kikimora and the injured fawn. The narrative tactfully portrays Geralt's empathy, suggesting that beneath the veneer of a monster hunter, there exists a capacity for compassion and an acknowledgment of the interconnectedness of life.

These events act as a narrative crucible, forging Geralt's identity as a morally gray and balanced character. His selective approach to killing, emphasis on dialogue and warnings, and moments of empathy underscore the depth and complexity of his moral framework. This phase sets the stage for further exploration of Geralt's character, inviting players and viewers to contemplate the shades of morality in *The Witcher*'s world. As Geralt becomes a father, having claimed the Law of Surprise when saving Emhyr of Cintra, he accepts the consequences of his decision. The narrative follows Geralt's journey as he raises Ciri as a human witcher, teaching her about the dichotomy of his foundational principle while sparing her the painful rites.

PARENTAL RESPONSIBILITY AND CIRI

Geralt's role as Ciri's father figure introduces another layer of moral complexity. The Law of Surprise binds them, setting the stage for moral dilemmas related to parental responsibility, sacrifice, and the consequences of the choices made for the well-being of another. How this furthers or hinders his growth toward the pinnacle of self-actualization depends significantly on the arc of sending Ciri away and the joy of reunion, the pain of sacrifice, and the ultimate realization that he has raised her to make the same painful choices he made, to protect or destroy.

Geralt's metamorphosis into a father figure for Ciri introduces profound moral intricacies, elevating the narrative's emotional and ethical complexity. The foundation of it lies in Geralt's decision to claim the Law of Surprise. As Geralt undertakes the responsibility of raising Ciri, he holds to the balance of keeping his word against the unthoughtful claim of the Law of Surprise. While rooted in tradition and fate, this decision thrusts Geralt into a role he may not have anticipated, unraveling a tapestry of challenges and moral quandaries. The theme of parental responsibility takes center stage, forcing Geralt to confront the weighty decisions inherent in guiding and safeguarding the life of another.

A central tension emerges as Geralt strives to strike a delicate equilibrium, resulting in a focal point for exploring the moral implications of his choices, reflecting the perennial struggle between duty and a paternal instinct to protect. The nuanced portrayal of this struggle invites contemplation on the broader themes of agency, autonomy, and the ethical dimensions of fostering individual growth.

Geralt's decision to deny Ciri the transformative rites inherent in becoming a full-fledged witcher manifests as a pivotal moral crossroads. While motivated by a desire to spare Ciri significant sacrifices and potential suffering and even death, this decision underscores his profound internal conflict. The moral implications resonate as Geralt grapples with the tension between his duty to uphold tradition and the paternal instinct to shield Ciri from unnecessary pain. Should he further the witcher's lineage? Should he risk the life of the child he feels the need to protect? He denies this rite, knowing it could either kill Ciri or propel her into safety and danger all at once. Finding that her heritage is not entirely human adds to the dilemma of making a one-of-a-kind elven-blood witcher or seeing the devastating ending to a promising life.

IS THERE A PRECISE ANSWER?

Geralt's struggle between duty and personal compassion becomes emblematic of the complex moral landscape that defines the world of *The Witcher*. The narrative masterfully navigates the tensions between tradition and individual well-being, prompting players and viewers to explore the ethical dimensions inherent in Geralt's choices as a surrogate father.

Exploring Geralt's role as a father figure to Ciri adds layers of moral complexity to *The Witcher*'s narrative tapestry. The interweaving themes of parental responsibility, sacrifice, and the consequences of decisions made for the well-being of another contribute to the rich moral fabric of the story, inviting audiences to grapple with the intricate moral quandaries that define Geralt's journey as a father in a world of monsters and men.

 ## THE VALUE OF *THE WITCHER* IN PERSONAL EXPLORATION

Geralt's character serves as a valuable framework for exploring moral development, choices, and consequences in therapeutic contexts. By delving into the multifaceted nature of Geralt's views and experiences, individuals can facilitate meaningful discussions that resonate with their personal journeys, fostering self-discovery and ethical growth.

The exploration of Geralt's character and values extends into the realm of personal awareness, presenting a multifaceted perspective that can be leveraged to assist individuals in navigating their moral dilemmas and personal development. The three distinct views of Geralt—the carefree wanderer (View 1), the duty-bound individual (View 2), and the professional (View 3)—offer rich insights into various approaches to healing and the creation of a personal moral code within everyday settings.

View 1, which portrays Geralt as a carefree wanderer seeking freedom, raises pertinent questions about the impact of rigid standards and the consequences of craving freedom without fully understanding its associated responsibilities. Individuals who have been subjected to tight control, such as those affected by religious trauma, may resonate with this view. Exploring this perspective allows people to delve into the implications of seeking freedom without recognizing the potential consequences, fostering discussions about the balance between freedom and accountability.

View 2, presenting Geralt as a duty-bound individual following strict guidelines of good versus evil, sheds light on the significance of adherence to moral codes and the implications of a structured approach to life. individuals who have experienced trauma or seek to understand their authentic selves may find resonance with this view. Anyone can use this perspective to explore the impact of strict standards on an individual's identity and how the quest for authenticity may align with or challenge these established norms.

View 3 emphasizes Geralt's professionalism, portraying him as a professional rather than a conventional hero. This view introduces the concept of universal ethics, where decisions are guided by a broader understanding of morality that transcends simplistic distinctions between good and evil. This perspective can encourage individuals to adopt a more comprehensive and nuanced approach to their moral decision-making in daily contexts. Geralt's ability to make choices based on universal ethics provides a framework for people to discuss the importance of considering broader implications and long-term consequences.

Geralt's experiences, including his role as a father figure to Ciri, can give insights into how therapists can guide clients through moral complexities related to parental responsibility, sacrifice, and the consequences of choices made for the well-being of others. By exploring these themes, individuals are provided context in how to navigate their own familial and interpersonal challenges, drawing parallels between Geralt's decisions and their own experiences.

The narrative also underscores Geralt's universal ethics, showcasing scenarios in the game where he makes choices based on a broader understanding of morality. This provides a foundation to discuss the significance of considering universal ethics in decision-making, urging people to move beyond narrow perspectives and embrace a more comprehensive view.

 CONCLUSION

Geralt's moral ambiguity and the dilemmas he faces contribute to the richness of *The Witcher* series. His character challenges conventional notions of heroism, emphasizing the complexity of morality in a world filled with monsters, humans, and everything in between. Whether making choices in gameplay or dealing with the consequences of his past, Geralt's character stands as a compelling exploration of the gray areas that define our decisions and shape our understanding of right and wrong.

About the Author

LOU ANNA CLAVEAU, MS, LPC has been in private practice since her graduation from Jacksonville State University with a Masters of Science degree since December of 2003. Mrs. Claveau has been an avid gamer of both TTRPGs and video games since 1978 when her brother invited both of his sisters to "play a game" at a local gamestore. Mist Foxwave a cleric, fighter, magic-user half-elf opened a world that helped Mrs. Claveau make it through some tough times. Mist runs a castle with her friends Ora, Zir and Tanlidge after defeating a lich and a five headed hydra in Dwarf Home. These interactions lead her to know the value gaming in real-life experiences as well as just having a good time. She now assists clients in the same way as a Certified Therapeutic Game Master through Geek Therapeutics. Weaving Monty Python, Shakespeare, Barbie and the lore of the "It's a Gazebo!" into treatment she now adds *The Witcher* to her bag of holding.

References

Bergen, Doris, and Darrel R. Davis 'Play Groups as Contexts for Moral Development,' in Lene

Arnett Jensen (ed.), *The Oxford Handbook of Moral Development: An Interdisciplinary Perspective*, Oxford Library of Psychology (2020; online edn, Oxford Academic, 5 Feb. 2020), https://doi.org/10.1093/oxfordhb/9780190676049.013.29

Cabellos B, Pozo J-I. Can Video Games Promote Moral Cognition? Supporting Epistemic Play

in *Papers, Please* through Dialogue. *Education Sciences*. 2023; 13(9):929. https://doi.org/10.3390/educsci13090929

Cherry, Kendra, 'Kohlbergs Theory of Moral Development' (updated September 2022)VeryWellMind.

https://www.verywellmind.com/kohlbergs-theory-of-moral-development-2795071

Ellemers, N., van der Toorn, J., Paunov, Y., & van Leeuwen, T. (2019). The Psychology of

Morality: A Review and Analysis of Empirical Studies Published From 1940 Through 2017. Personality and Social Psychology Review, 23(4), 332–366. https://doi.org/10.1177/1088868318811759

Fatima Malik; Raman Marwaha. Developmental Stages of Social Emotional Development in

Children. (September 18, 2022) National Library of Medicine.

https://www.ncbi.nlm.nih.gov/books/NBK534819/

Hodge SE, Taylor J, McAlaney J. It's Double-Edged: The Positive and Negative Relationships

Between the Development of Moral Reasoning and Video Game Play Among Adolescents. Front Psychol. 2019 Jan 22;10:28. doi: 10.3389/fpsyg.2019.00028. PMID: 30740072; PMCID: PMC6357883.

Iordanis Kavathatzopoulos (1991) Kohlberg and Piaget: differences and similarities, Journal

of Moral Education, 20:1, 47–54, DOI: 10.1080/0305724910200104

McLeod, Saul, 'Kohlberg's Theory Of Moral Development' (updated January 2024) Simply

Psychology. https://www.simplypsychology.org/kohlberg.html

McLeod, Saul, 'Piaget's Theory Of Moral Development' (updated 2023) Simply Psychology.

https://www.simplypsychology.org/piaget-moral.html

Serhat, Kurt. 'Stages of Moral Development – Lawrence Kohlberg' (August 17, 2020)

Educational Technology. https://educationaltechnology.net/stages-of-moral-development-lawrence-kohlberg/

"Bystander Effect." Psychology Today, accessed June 2024, https://www.psychologytoday.com/us/basics/bystander-effect.

7

SEARCHING FOR CONNECTION: TYPES OF LOVE IN *THE WITCHER*

WENDI "NICKI" LINE

In this crazy world, full of change and chaos, there is
one thing of which I am certain, one thing which does
not change: my love for you

— Geralt

E xploring the vast world of *The Witcher*, whether through its books, games, or television adaptation, reveals a poignant theme deeply rooted in human experience: the inherent longing for connection and belonging. This theme mirrors the fundamental human need for love and acceptance, as outlined by Maslow's Hierarchy of Needs. Within the intricate societal tapestry portrayed in the Witcherverse, interpersonal connections are not merely optional but essential for survival in its harsh, archaic settings. Families, alliances, and bonds formed through shared endeavors are not luxuries but vital for navigating a world fraught with danger and intrigue. However, amid the characters' trials and tribulations, *The Witcher* reaches beyond mere survival instincts, exploring the multifaceted nature of love and relationships.

Within the Witcherverse, characters like Geralt, Yennefer, Ciri, and Jaskier embark not only on personal quests but also a search for belonging, forging chosen families built on the pillars of friendship and familial love. These bonds, rooted in the Greek concept of storge, reflect the complexities outlined in Lee's Color Wheel and Sternberg's Triangle of Love theories, where intimacy, passion, and commitment intertwine to create various forms of love. Consider Geralt's dynamic with Yennefer, evolving from infatuated love to consummate love—a blend of passion and deep connection. Conversely, Geralt's relationship with Jaskier epitomizes companionate love, shown through enduring commitment and intimacy. *The Witcher*'s exploration of these diverse types of love enriches its narrative, offering a profound reflection on the human condition, emphasizing the universal need for meaningful connections, and belonging within a group.

Understanding the intricacies of relationships within the Witcherverse necessitates grasping relationship theories, providing a framework for dissecting the multifaceted dynamics at play. Through its portrayal of love in its myriad forms, *The Witcher* invites audiences to contemplate the depths of human connection and the profound significance of belonging—to a family, to a community, and ultimately, to one another.

MASLOW'S HIERARCHY OF NEEDS

Self-Actualization
Realizing your full potential "becoming everything one is capable of becoming."

Aesthetic Needs
Beauty-in art and nature- symmetry, balance, order, and form.

Cognitive Needs
Knowledge and understanding, curiousity, exploration, need for meaning and predictability.

Esteem Needs
The esteem and respect of other and self esteem and self respect. A self of competence.

Love and Belonging
Giving and recieving love, affection, trust, and acceptance. Affliating, being a part of a group (friends, family, work)

Safety Needs
Protection from potentially dangerous objects or situations, e.g. the elements, phyiscal illness. The threat is both phyiscal and psychological, (e.g. "fear of the unknown"). Importance of routine and familiarity.

Survival /Physiological Needs
Food, drink, oxygen, temperature regulation, elimination, rest, activity, sex

Figure 1 – Maslow's Hierarchy of Needs extended version

Regardless of its version, Maslow's Hierarchy of Needs encompasses a spectrum ranging from survival to self-actualization or transcendence, as seen in its extended form. Positioned above survival and safety needs are love and belongingness, or social needs, constituting the third level. At this stage, the intrinsic drive for emotional relationships and a sense of belonging within a community propels human behavior. Various types of relationships fulfill this need, including friendships, romantic attachments, family ties, social groups, community involvement, and participation in spiritual organizations. Being part of a group serves as a buffer against loneliness, depression, and anxiety. Personal connections with friends, family, and romantic partners are crucial, as is engagement in broader social circles. A 2020 study on college students underscored a positive correlation between a sense of belonging, heightened happiness, and overall well-being, revealing a notable decrease in mental health disorders such as anxiety, depression, hopelessness, loneliness, social anxiety, and suicidal ideation among those who felt a strong sense of belonging. In the archaic setting of the Witcherverse, a sense of community and belonging proves indispensable.

Fans of *The Witcher* keenly observe characters actively searching for a sense of belonging. For example, Geralt of Rivia, firmly rooted in the witcher fraternity, finds this affiliation insufficient to fulfill all his social needs, particularly regarding romantic and familial love. Yennefer of Vengerberg, propelled by her pursuit of power, also seeks a community to belong to, initially finding solace in the Aretuza School for Sorceresses. However, disillusioned by the emptiness of her quest for power, she ultimately yearns for a familial bond of her own. Ciri Riannon, once a princess of Cintra, grapples with the loss of her family following the invasion by the Nilfgaardian Empire, leaving her exiled and adrift. Amid her struggle for survival and security, she seeks belongingness, finding it with Geralt and briefly with the Rat gang. Finally, Julian Alfred Pankratz, Viscount de Lettenhove, better known as Dandelion or Jaskier, embarks on a quest for fame, eventually discovering camaraderie within the company of Geralt, Yennefer, and Ciri. Each character, whether consciously aware or not, desires to be part of something greater than themselves, driving their actions and choices throughout their respective journeys. In Season 3, Episode 4 of the Netflix series *The Witcher*, titled "The Invitation," viewers witness an example of such a moment among the four main characters before Geralt and Yennefer embark on their journey to the ball and conclave. These scenes showcase intimate inside jokes shared between Ciri and Jaskier, often at Geralt's expense, highlighting the camaraderie and closeness that develops within tight-knit groups. The expressions of love depicted vary depending on the individual needs within these relationships, a concept that John Alan Lee further explores in his Color Wheel Theory of Love.

 COLOR WHEEL THEORY OF LOVE

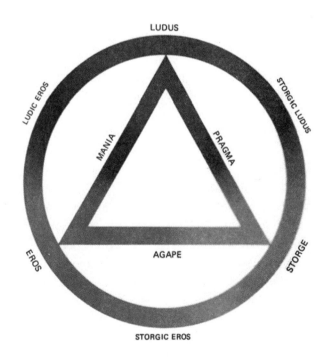

Figure 2

Canadian psychologist John Alan Lee revolutionized the understanding of love with his color wheel theory, delineating fifteen distinct types rooted in Latin and Greek terminology. Lee categorizes these into three primary, three secondary, and nine tertiary love styles, employing the traditional color wheel as a framework. This chapter focuses on the exploration and illustration of the three primary types—eros, ludus, and storge—within the context of the Witcherverse, offering insightful examples that illuminate the nuances of these fundamental forms of love.

Eros

Often synonymous with romantic love, eros finds its origins in Greek mythology as a manifestation of madness triggered by Cupid's arrow. This form of love is characterized by intense passion and desire, as vividly depicted in stories such as Paris and Helen, which ultimately resulted in the downfall of Troy. In contemporary society, eros intertwines with the primal instincts of survival and reproduction, with individuals driven by eros often viewing marriage as an eternal honeymoon and regarding sex as a deeply profound spiritual experience.

Those enveloped by eros tend to idolize their partners, yearning to share every facet of their lives and often perceiving them through a rosy lens. Criticism from their beloved can deeply wound them, and the mere thought of separation can evoke agonizing emotions. In *The Witcher 3: The Wild Hunt*, players encounter a romance option with Triss Marigold, a sorceress akin to Yennefer. The relationship between Geralt and Triss mirrors the intense, almost fairy-tale connection suggesting eros love, potentially culminating in settling down in Kovir and enjoying a blissful life together.

The advantage of eros lies in the profound emotional bond it fosters between partners, wherein feelings of lust and love mutually reinforce each other, providing a greater sense of security and purpose in life. However, sustaining eros necessitates concerted effort from both partners to maintain sexual interest and nurture the health of the relationship. One downside is the risk of fostering unrealistic expectations, potentially leading to a decline in attraction over time. At its extreme, eros can breed naivety, and partners who are less inclined toward sexual intimacy may feel undervalued and objectified within the relationship dynamic. The viewers do not see the total progression of Geralt and Triss's relationship and are unable to witness the effort and overall wellness.

Ludus

Derived from the Latin word for "game" or "school," ludus characterizes a love style where individuals perceive relationships as avenues for fun and amusement. They relish engaging in activities, teasing, and playing pranks with their partners, viewing love and attention as components of a playful game. Their priority lies in enjoying themselves, and they may not necessarily pursue committed relationships. Jaskier epitomizes ludic love through his carefree approach to sex and relationships. Throughout the Netflix series, he boasts about his sexual escapades and playful nature, often landing himself in trouble with jealous partners or spouses. As with most ludic lovers, Jaskier tends to conceal his true thoughts and feelings, especially if he believes it could offer him an advantage. Moreover, ludic lovers might engage in consensual nonmonogamy, maintaining multiple partners simultaneously, albeit with the inherent risk of infidelity unless all parties involved agree to nonmonogamous arrangements.

Storge

Meaning familial love in Greek, storge is described by Lee as a love that grows gradually out of friendship, emphasizing shared interests and commitment over passion. It encompasses the love between siblings, spouses, cousins, parents, and children, and is characterized by familial loyalty, responsibility, and mutual support. Family members prioritize each other's well-being and often form a sanctuary within the home. Characters in *The Witcher* such as Ciri, Yennefer, Geralt, and Jaskier exemplify storgic love through their enduring bonds despite facing betrayals and hardships. A prime example is found in an episode titled "The Invitation." A scene shows Ciri and Yennefer reconciling after a conflict, apologizing, and acknowledging each other's roles in the issue. This moment illustrates Lee's concept of storgic love, where mutual understanding and support strengthen familial bonds over time. In many cases, storgic love develops from long-standing relationships or cohabitation, evolving from friendship or extended time spent together, and is known to endure beyond the dissolution of a romantic relationship.

John Alan Lee's Color Wheel Theory of Love provides an insightful framework for understanding the complexities of love, categorizing it into primary styles such as eros, ludus, and storge, among others. However, as the understanding of love evolves, Robert Sternberg's Triangular Theory of Love offers a complementary perspective, delving deeper into the dynamics of relationships much like the affection between Geralt and Yennefer. Sternberg's theory introduces three fundamental components of love: intimacy, passion, and commitment, forming various combinations that define different types of love, including consummate love, companionate love, and infatuation. Transitioning from Lee's Color Wheel to Sternberg's Triangle offers a richer understanding of the complex nature of love, encompassing both its emotional spectrum and structural elements as depicted in the Witcherverse.

TRIANGULAR THEORY OF LOVE

Sternberg's Triangle Theory of Love

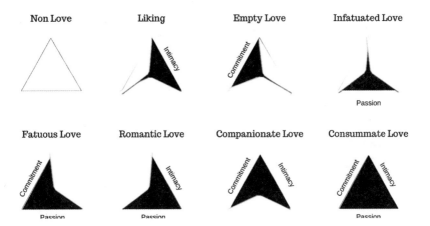

Figure 3 Sternberg's 8 types of love in the Triangle Theory of Love

In 1986, Sternberg introduced his triangular theory of love, outlining three components that combine in various ways to form eight types of love. These components are intimacy, passion, and decision/commitment.

Intimacy refers to feelings of closeness, connection, and emotional investment in a relationship. It remains relatively stable over time, though awareness of these feelings may fluctuate. Intimacy plays a more significant role in long-term relationships and generates a moderate psychophysiological response, as seen in the relationship between the four main characters.

Passion encompasses romantic feelings, physical attraction, and sexual desire such as Jaskier's developing relationship with Prince Radovid. It tends to be unstable and can fluctuate, leading to a high psychophysiological response. Passion plays a larger role in short-term relationships.

Decision/commitment involves the decision to love someone and the commitment to maintain that love over time. It is more easily controlled than intimacy and remains consistent over time. Decision/commitment plays a larger role in long-term relationships, ensuring their continuity. Geralt chooses commitment when he embraces Ciri as his Child of Surprise and continues to work on improving their bond.

An imbalance in these components can lead to unfulfilling relationships. For instance, romantic love may lack commitment, or companionate love may lack passion. True consummate love is achieved when all three components are present and balanced. Understanding Sternberg's theory helps explain the dynamics of different types of love and how they evolve in relationships within the Witcherverse.

Nonlove

Sternberg's first type of love, nonlove, describes relationships where none of the three components of love—intimacy, passion, or commitment—are present. According to Sternberg, nonlove is common in our everyday interactions and characterizes most of our personal relationships. These interactions lack any form of love, as none of the components are evident. Many of the companions of the main characters fall into this category. Characters like Queen Calanthe, Fiona Riannon of Cintra, and sorceress Philippa have relationships with Geralt and Yennefer characterized by nonlove. There is no loyalty, passion, or intimacy between Geralt and Yennefer and these characters. Their interactions are brief and lack any depth of emotional connection.

Liking/Friendship

The second type of love Sternberg discusses is liking or friendship, where the intimacy component of love is present, but passion and commitment are absent. In liking, individuals feel a sense of closeness and warmth toward each other, akin to friendship, but without the intense passion or long-term commitment found in other types of love. True liking exists when friendships lack both passion and commitment in the triangle of love. Geralt, Jaskier, and Zoltan Chivay exemplify this type of connection. Zoltan, a dwarf entrepreneur and veteran of battles, shares a deep friendship with Geralt and Jaskier. Their bond formed years ago during a chance encounter across war stricken Riverdell, and while they share camaraderie and closeness, their relationship lacks the romantic passion or long-term commitment found in other types of love.

Infatuation

The third type of love Sternberg identifies is infatuation, characterized by the presence of passion but the absence of intimacy and commitment. This love is often associated with whirlwind romances driven by intense passion but lacking in deeper emotional connection or long-term commitment. Sternberg places "love at first sight" within this category, describing it as a sudden and intense attraction marked by high levels of physiological arousal, such as increased heart rate and hormonal secretions. Infatuated love develops rapidly, without allowing time for intimacy to grow or commitment to form. Viewers witness instances of infatuated love with Geralt's quick romances or one-night stands. In the books, Geralt's relationship with Triss Marigold is marked by Triss's initial curiosity about Geralt's love for Yennefer. She seduces Geralt with a spell to experience his love, but her feelings quickly develop into infatuation. Similarly, Geralt's brief love affair with Renfri can be seen as infatuated in nature. Jaskier and Yennefer similarly depict whirlwind romances, characterized by intense passion but lacking depth or commitment.

Empty Love

When the commitment component is present, with the absence of intimacy and passion, it is categorized as empty love. This type of love is often observed in long-term relationships where the initial feelings of closeness and passion have faded away. Interestingly, Sternberg notes in our society, empty love is seen as a final or near-final stage in a relationship; in other cultures, it may be the initial stage, such as in arranged marriages. Arranged marriages are prevalent in the Witcherverse, since its societal structure is similar to medieval Europe. In the first season of the Netflix series, Queen Calanthe of Cintra seeks betrothals for her daughter, Pavetta, and her granddaughter, Princess Ciri, to form political alliances with other nations. In such arrangements, the commitment to the marriage may exist, but the emotional intimacy and passion between the partners may initially be lacking.

Romantic Love

The fifth type of love in the triangle is romantic love, characterized by the presence of intimacy and passion but lacking commitment. This type of love combines the warmth and closeness of liking with the intense feelings of physical attraction. Sternberg notes that romantic love often occurs in the early stages of a relationship, before the partners have made a long-term commitment to each other. A prime example of romantic love is seen in the relationship between Geralt and Yennefer. Initially, they share deep feelings of intimacy and passion, but they have not yet made a formal commitment to each other. As their relationship progresses, they eventually move toward consummate love, where all three components of love—intimacy, passion, and commitment—are present.

Companionate Love

On Sternberg's triangle of love, companionate love is marked by intimacy and commitment without passion. It mirrors a long-term, committed friendship, notably seen in marriages where initial physical attraction wanes over time. Similarly, in the Witcherverse, Geralt and Jaskier epitomize companionate love; though Geralt may lack passionate feelings for Jaskier, there exists a profound intimacy and commitment between them. Fans can discern the tension and allure Jaskier holds for Geralt, despite the absence of romantic reciprocity. This depth of passion forms the central theme of Jaskier's primary ballad in Season 2, "Burn Witcher Burn," reflecting on the nonromantic nature of their relationship.

Fatuous Love

Sternberg's fatuous love is characterized by passion and commitment but lacking in intimacy and deep understanding. This type of love often emerges quickly, based on intense physical and romantic attraction, without the foundation of a strong emotional connection. Fatuous love is sometimes associated with Hollywood portrayals or whirlwind courtships, where couples rush into marriage without allowing time for the development of true intimacy. This is very true in the first season's "Of Banquets, Bastards, and Burials," where it is revealed Pavetta, Ciri's mother, developed a whirlwind romance with Duny. The two depict their commitment and passion for one another, as evident in the ballroom scene during the Child of Surprise revelation for both Duny and Geralt. Because these relationships lack the stabilizing element of emotional involvement, they are more prone to failure. This is evident in the rumors in the the Netflix series of Pavetta's murder as a result of Duny's ambition to rule Nilfgaard and anger at leaving Ciri in Cintra.

Consummate Love

The eighth and final type of love within Sternberg's triangle is consummate love, which represents the ideal form of love where all three components are present in a relationship. In contemporary society consummate love is considered the most complete and balanced form of love, embodying deep connection and understanding, physical and romantic attraction, and a long-term commitment to maintaining the relationship. Geralt and Yennefer especially demonstrate consummate love with the addition of romantic elements, showcasing a deep and balanced connection that encompasses all three components of love. Outside of romantic contexts, consummate love is observed in the unconditional love caregivers feel for their children. The four main characters in *The Witcher* exemplify consummate love in their relationships. The bond between Geralt, Yennefer, Ciri, and Jaskier reflects a chosen family dynamic where they commit to each other, continually strive to know each other intimately, and share a nonromantic physical attraction to be close with one another.

CONCLUSION

In conclusion, the Witcherverse masterfully showcases the significance of connection and the diversity of relationships in harsh settings, resonating across various media platforms. These portrayals not only provide valuable insights into viewers' own relationships but also contribute to their self-awareness, drawing parallels with psychological theories like Maslow's Hierarchy of Needs, the color wheel theory, and the triangular theory of love. Through research, introspection, and seeking professional guidance, individuals can deepen their understanding of themselves and make informed choices in nurturing meaningful relationships.

The depiction of healthy relationships in the Witcherverse offers a beacon of inspiration, motivating viewers to actively seek and cultivate similar connections in their own lives, thereby enriching their overall well-being and fulfillment.

About the Author

WENDI "NICKI" LINE, LMHC, CGT is a licensed mental health clinician and a board certified sex therapist in Florida. She completed her masters degree at Liberty University in Lynchburg, VA. Nicki provides care for clients in private practice using an eclectic style. She works primarily with relationships and families. Her niches include trauma, addiction, relationships, sex, LGBTQ+, consensual non-monogamy, kink, and geek culture. Nicki has provided several professional trainings, including The Supernatural Mental Health series for Geek Therapeutics.

References

Anderson, J. W. (2016). Sternberg's triangular theory of Love. Encyclopedia of Family Studies, 1–3. https://doi.org/10.1002/9781119085621.wbefs058

CD Projekt Red, Breakpoint, Can Explode Games, Fuero Games, & Spokko. (2007, October 26). The Witcher. Computer software. Retrieved 2021.

Halwani, R. (2018). Philosophy of love, sex, and marriage an introduction. Routledge.

Hissrich, L. S. (2019, December 20). The Witcher, The Ends Beginning. Whole.

Holler, M. (2023). Structured Relationship Theory: Nothing less would have sufficed. AR Press.

Lee, J. A. (1976). The colors of Love. Bantam Books.

Mustofa, A. Z. (2022). Hierarchy of human needs: A humanistic psychology approach of Abraham Maslow. Kawanua International Journal of Multicultural Studies, 3(2), 30–35. https://doi.org/10.30984/kijms.v3i2.282

Oghia, M. (2011). Sternberg Triangle Theory of Love. LOVEanon. Retrieved January 22, 2024, from https://www.loveanon.org/2011/09/theory-of-love-pt-2-sternbergs.html.

Sapkowski, A., & French, D. (2023). Sword of destiny. Gollancz.

Sapkowski, A., & Stok, D. (2017). Blood of elves. Orbit.

Sapkowski, A., & Stok, D. (2023). The last wish. Gollancz.

Varden, H. (2020). Sexual and affectionate love. Sex, Love, and Gender, 33–78. https://doi.org/10.1093/oso/9780198812838.003.0003

Zurenko, K. D. (2015). Color Wheel of Love. Wikipedia. photograph. Retrieved January 22, 2024, from https://en.wikipedia.org/wiki/Colour_wheel_theory_of_love#/media/File:Colour_Wheel_of_Love.jpeg.

8

FOUR PHASES OF YENNEFER: SELF-DETERMINATION THEORY AND YENNEFER'S PERSONAL DEVELOPMENT

JOE LECONTE

"Remember... magic is Chaos, Art and Science. It is a curse, a blessing and progress. It all depends on who uses magic, how they use it, and to what purpose. And magic is everywhere. All around us. Easily accessible."

— Yennefer

Yennefer of Vengerberg has had a rough life. Born to a farmer who sold her for four marks, she survived attacks from a djinn, a fire mage, a bug monster, and the entire Nilfgaardian army. Yet, she began her life as a "crooked girl" with a curved spine and became one of the most powerful mages ever to live on the Continent. How did this happen?

To understand her life, it helps to understand her motivations. Yennefer's life is broken up into four key phases within the first two seasons of the *Witcher* television show. Viewing her experience with the added knowledge of Self-Determination Theory can help provide clarity to the choices she makes along the way.

The Self-Determination Theory (SDT) was first developed by Richard Ryan and Edward Deci in 1985. Ryan and Deci's model can be defined in several key terms that are relevant to Yennefer. Specifically, SDT implies that all people have three basic needs: autonomy, competence, and connection.

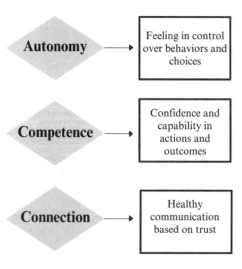

Figure 1

These needs are fulfilled by choices that are autonomous or controlled. An autonomous motivation comes from within a person and is not influenced by external factors. Autonomous motivations come from internal codes of conduct or morality that are developed over a lifetime of experiences, unlike controlled motivations which are the result of rewards or consequences from external groups and standards such as obligations to a religious order, a military code of conduct, or an agreement with an employer.

Throughout Yennefer's life she strives to be free from control of various influences such as the Brotherhood of Sorcerers or Voleth Meir. Her desire for competence drives her during her magical training and pushes her toward seemingly reckless uses of her power when she defeats the army of Nilfgaard. Yennefer's desire for connection is more complex. For most of her life she desires power and all the associated credibility and status that comes with it. Few people get close to Yennefer; she's always kept her guard up. Her competence always seemed to get in the way of connection.

According to SDT, the desires for autonomy, competence, and connection may be Yennefer's goal. Yet how she chooses to pursue those needs affect her decision-making. SDT provides a framework to examine these motivations. According to Ryan and Deci, people generally experience three types of motivation: amotivation, external motivation, and intrinsic motivation.

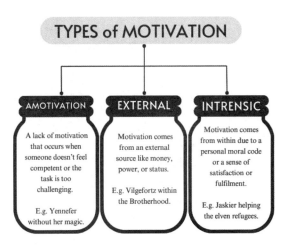

Figure 2

Amotivation and intrinsic motivation don't have variable states the way external motivation does. Within extrinsic motivation there are several different types of regulation that change a person's motivations. This spectrum of external regulation is defined by a mini-theory within SDT called Organismic Integration Theory

(OIT). According to OIT, there are four different types of external motivation: external, introjected, identified, and integrated.

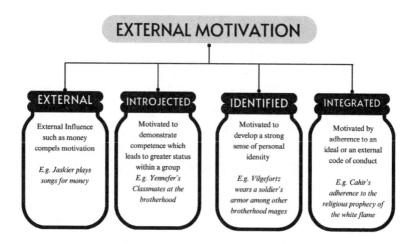

Figure 3

Within SDT, many of the different motivations and regulations may appear to occur on a spectrum or on a scale, that is to say, with amotivation being at the bottom of a scale and intrinsic motivation being at the top with extrinsic motivation in between. It is important to understand that SDT is not a staged theory; a person does not begin their motivation at amotivation and develop through external motivation to achieve intrinsic motivation. These different motivations can exist separately and simultaneously within people, and may change over time. Yennefer's journey from tormented child to beloved magical tutor provides a clear journey through all three forms of motivation. For Yennefer, the pursuit of her three needs—autonomy, connectedness and competence—determine her goals during the various phases of her life. Yennefer is a complex person, but in the world of *The Witcher*, destiny is often credited with the choices different characters make.

Is destiny alone sufficient to explain the complexities of a person like Yennefer of Vengerberg?

PHASE 1: INTROJECTED REGULATION — SEASON 1, EPISODES 2-4

Yennefer's choices come from her desire to identify as a capable student of the Brotherhood of Sorcerers.

Yennefer's motivations in the beginning of her time with the Brotherhood are introjected. She is motivated to become the best student she can. Examining her choices using SDT's ideas of autonomous vs. controlled motivations can help to understand the situation. Yennefer's choices are clearly generated from an external controlled source. Her identity as a student in the Brotherhood of Sorcerers gives her a framework to identify aspects of herself that she values and other aspects that she wants to change. As she becomes more competent as a student, her sense of introjected regulation helps to reinforce the decisions she is making in order to gain status within the organization.

According to SDT, her three basic needs in this period would be filled by her desire to develop her identity as a successful student. Her magical studies under Tissaia don't initially progress as quickly as her peers, but she builds her competence over time. She can move about the new magical compound of Aretuza at her discretion, providing her a sense of autonomy. She knows that she doesn't trust Tissaia but she feels a strong connection to Istredd.

Throughout her time as a student, Yennefer struggles, and her competence is challenged. Be it through lifting a rock without touching it or bottling lightning, she has to work hard. Eventually, she witnesses her less capable peers become transformed into magical eels that power Aretuza. This event is the final piece of proof that Yennefer needs to show that her struggles have not been in vain.

At this phase in her life, Yennefer's methods of decision-making have helped her to develop her skills as a student and reinforced the introjected regulation that she has relied upon, albeit unconsciously, to feel secure in her identity as well as satisfy her three basic needs. While the lessons she learned at Aretuza may have been abusive and traumatic, her motivation is firmly planted in the desire to develop status within a specific social framework. She expresses validation of her choices upon the arrival of initiation day, telling Istredd, "After initiation today, we're in charge. We get to make the decisions and be who we want to be." Yennefer is unable to see beyond the institution of the Brotherhood. Her decision-making functions only as an extension of the values she has learned from being a student. Her introjected regulation allows her to rationalize many of the decisions she makes, in her pursuit of meeting her needs. However, her introjected regulation stops her from recognizing situations that can be dangerous, or in one case, extremely traumatizing.

INTROJECTED REGULATION

"After initiation today, we're in charge. We get to make the decisions and be who we want to be."

Yennefer's physical differences do not hold her back from becoming a capable mage. Yet, as her initiation into the Brotherhood draws near, she meets a character called the enchanter. He relies on Yennefer's desire for competence and connection to promote an ideal of physical beauty that the Brotherhood enforces with their students. The audience watches Yennefer struggle with her decision to adhere to the ideal of conventional beauty. The enchanter tells Yennefer, "You can free the victim in the mirror forever." His words prey upon Yennefer's desire for her needs to be met and draws associations of competence being associated with conventional beauty. As part of her initiation into the ranks of the Brotherhood, Yennefer has been led to believe that her needs will be fulfilled as long as she is a successful student and can consistently demonstrate competence. She believes she will be assigned to the kingdom of Aedirn. Her competence has all but guaranteed her the position. Yet somehow, she is assigned to Nilfgaard, a frigid, undesirable backwater that she has no interest in. Yennefer is left with a choice: accept her assignment or conform to the expectations of the Brotherhood and become conventionally beautiful to woo the king of Aedirn.

When a person's decision-making is external and introjected, they develop expectations that the choices they make to meet their needs must fit within the established norms of the organization they believe is important. Yennefer's desire for status within the Brotherhood means she will make choices that affect her position in a desired or undesired way.

Yennefer's introjected regulation of being the best student possible allows her to rationalize her decision to go through with the enchanter's procedure. This is the highest point of her introjected regulation. When she demands to go through the enchantment and make herself conventionally beautiful, she also accepts that the enchantment requires the removal of her ability to bear children. Yennefer's uterus is removed and used as a spell component for a successful but brutal transformation into a conventionally beautiful woman. Yet she chooses to retain two aspects of her old physical form: her eyes remain the same, as a way to call attention to her elven heritage and thumb her nose in the face of the Brotherhood's attempt to use her elven blood against her. She also chooses to retain the scars on her wrists from her suicide attempt. The choice to keep her scars intact has nothing to do with the Brotherhood. Instead, they are a reminder of her competence and how far she has come since beginning her education. They act as a reminder of her lowest point and offer a very small amount of intrinsic motivation.

Yennefer's choice to retain these parts of her own identity illustrates an important distinction. SDT is not a model that exists on a spectrum. Yennefer's decision to defy the Brotherhood doesn't mean her motivation isn't introjected. She believes, based on her own morals, that her suicide attempt and her elven heritage are an important part of who she is, even if the Brotherhood does not. Yet she still wants to be a well-regarded student and develop a status commensurate with her abilities. Even though she is drawing attention to an aspect of her heritage by keeping her elven eyes, and maintaining the scars on her wrists in defiance of the ideals of conventional beauty, Yennefer is still focused on her status in the Brotherhood. The two motivations can exist simultaneously, according to SDT, but the introjected regulation is the more dominant, due to its greater influence on Yennefer's decision-making.

Thirty years after the procedure, Yennefer has maintained her introjected regulation as a dutiful student turned court mage. However, her high level of competence has given her the status she sought but left her bored and unfulfilled. Her role protecting Queen Kalis and her newborn daughter during a carriage ride is something that takes minimal effort. During the ride, Queen Kalis and Yennefer discuss her position as court mage. Kalis believes that Yennefer has made a wise choice to pursue magic and power, even at the cost of her own fertility. Kalis, by contrast, begrudgingly feels as though her only role in court is to produce a male heir for King Virfuril—a task that she has been unable to accomplish.

The conversation shows how two separate organizations can still create the circumstances for introjected regulation. Queen

Kalis exists within the social framework of the kingdom of Aedirn. Her competence is linked to her ability to give birth to a male heir. While she admires Yennefer's magical prowess at the cost of her fertility, she is still focusing her decision-making on status within an external organization. From the other side of the conversation, Yennefer's boredom with her role as court mage demonstrates some desire to find fulfillment outside of the Brotherhood, but her lack of life experience doesn't provide her with many options, so her regulation remains based within the Brotherhood.

Yennefer's considerations of changing her motivations are reinforced when she has to defend herself, Queen Kalis and her infant daughter from an assassin. Yennefer is able to save her own life but is unsuccessful in saving Kalis or her daughter.

With the dead infant in her arms, Yennefer reflects on her life over the last thirty years. She knows she is a capable sorcerer, but she questions why she is wasting her time working for an organization that has sent her to clean up messes for a king who tried to assassinate her. In her frustration, she tells the unnamed dead child that she is better off being dead. "We're still just vessels for them to take and take until we're empty and alone." She buries the body of the infant and sets off on a new phase of her life.

Why did Yennefer's motivation change? Was it the betrayal of the Brotherhood or King Virfuril? The assassination attempts certainly didn't endear Yennefer to either organization. One possible explanation for her change can be found in Cognitive Evaluation Theory (CET), a mini-theory within SDT. CET helps to define the factors that can increase or undermine a person's internal motivation. For example, if a person is provided rewards for certain behavior such as money, prizes, or something tangible, they are more likely to gain or maintain external motivation. If a person is rewarded with something intangible and desirable, like praise, they are more likely to gain or maintain internal motivation. However, if a person receives something undesirable intangible, like a threat, their sense of internal motivation is also diminished. In Yennefer's case, her rewards from the Brotherhood are tangible. Her magical abilities that she gains due to her time studying in Aretuza are a tangible reward for her efforts. Therefore, Yennefer's development of introjected regulation and desire to be well regarded within the social world of the Brotherhood make sense.

After Yennefer leaves the Brotherhood to work in Aedirn, she no longer receives those tangible rewards. Her magical skills stop developing, and she is given opportunities to make choices outside of her goal to be a successful student. After enough time has passed, she is able to see that the world outside of her magical studies has more to offer. As Yennefer walks away from her life as a mage of the Brotherhood, does she develop a greater intrinsic motivation? Not really.

PHASE 2: IDENTIFIED REGULATION — SEASON 1, EPISODES 5–8

Yennefer seeks to become a powerful independent mage and show that her skills are greater than any mage in the Brotherhood.

After her departure from the Brotherhood of Sorcerers, Yennefer is still externally motivated, but instead of introjected regulation leading her to be the most capable student in the Brotherhood, she has decided to amplify her sense of autonomy and become an independent sorcerer. She doesn't just want to be known as the best mage in the Brotherhood, she wants to be the most powerful mage anywhere.

SDT calls this identified regulation. Yennefer's new regulation is still external, much like her introjected regulation in the first phase of her life. But introjected regulation has caused Yennefer's behaviors to reflect a desire to avoid shame and improve feelings of pride in her skills as a mage. In the second phase of her life, Yennefer no longer values the Brotherhood's opinion of her. Her behavior is now focused on valuing her own pursuit of status in the larger world.

She lives and works on the outside of formalized Brotherhood society, however, she still evaluates her competence against the abilities of Brotherhood mages. Yennefer's value of magical ability is exemplified when the audience learns she is attempting to repair her body so she can have children. But does her desire to repair herself come from a desire for connection and a child, or is it to show competence beyond the Brotherhood?

Her determination to revive her fertility may partially be out of a desire to have a child, however, the majority of her motivation seems to come from a wish to prove that she can do something no other mage has done before. Yennefer's motivation seems to grow when she is contacted by Tissaia, who tells Yennefer if she keeps up her efforts to reverse her infertility, she will be targeted by the Brotherhood. Yennefer believes that Tissaia's threat is based on the potential to make the Brotherhood lose face. She tells Tissaia, "You only want me to do well so long as you have your hand in it." As Yennefer's status as an independent mage develops, she continues to measure her success based on the limits that were imposed on her by the Brotherhood when she was still a student.

IDENTIFIED REGULATION

"They took my choice. I want it back."

During the second phase of her life, Yennefer's three main needs of competence, connection, and autonomy are still present, as they are in all stages of regulation. However, she seeks to fulfill them in new ways. When Geralt and Yennefer first meet in Rinde, Yennefer has sets up a small business helping people with physical ailments, such as erectile dysfunction. This small amount of status is not nearly as significant as her previous assignment in Aedirn, but her desire for autonomy is fulfilled, as is her desire for the recognition of her competence in magic. Yet her sense of connection remains maladaptive. This becomes apparent when Geralt brings an injured Jaskir to the house Yennefer has taken over for herself. When she learns that Jaskir has been struck by dangerous magic from a djinn, Yennefer hatches her own plan to use the djinn's powerful magic to accomplish her goal of returning her fertility. This plan eventually fails, but Yennefer continues her efforts.

The next time the duo meet is when Yennefer and Geralt find themselves hunting for a dragon. Yennefer explains to Geralt that she wants to use the dragon's body to extract some kind of magical healing properties, continuing her quest to restore her fertility. During the conversation about the possibility of Yennefer being able to heal herself, she discloses to Geralt the true reason for her search for her body's autonomy: anger with the Brotherhood. "They took my choice. I want it back."

According to Deci and Ryan, "The term extrinsic motivation refers to the performance of an activity in order to attain some separable outcome and, thus, contrasts with intrinsic motivation, which refers to doing an activity for the inherent satisfaction of the activity itself." This choice to use the magic afflicting Jaskir or the body of a dragon is rational to Yennefer and demonstrates an external motivation.

If she is able to return her fertility, she will repair damage to herself that the Brotherhood has told her cannot be healed.

During their dragon hunt, Geralt asks Yennefer, "Did you always dream of becoming a mother?"

"I dreamed of becoming important to someone, someday."

Yennefer may have no desire at all to be a mother or achieve the type of connectedness with a child. It is likely, she wants to demonstrate a higher level of competence and prove Tissaia and the rest of the Brotherhood wrong by showing that she can succeed where none before her have. She will become the most powerful independent mage and be able to have children. Her desires come from an external place due to her desire to create a specific outcome that cannot be recognized without the Brotherhood. This is reinforced when Tissaia threatens her to stop. This is unlike introjected regulation, where Yennefer was forced to act within the confines of the Brotherhood; her goal of becoming powerful is her own.

Later, when the Brotherhood convinces Yennefer that Nilfgaard is a threat, and they need to fight back on behalf of the northern kingdoms, she agrees to join them at the Battle of Sodden Hill, but why? Yennefer no longer has anything to prove to the Brotherhood. Her sense of autonomy has been satisfied along with her need to be seen as competent enough to live outside of their organization.

When the Brotherhood of Sorcerers wants her back, her desire for the return of her fertility is forgotten. The dream she shared with Geralt has come true. She is important to someone, even if it is the group of mages who tormented her as a child. Her goal has been validated by the external force that she has been working to separate herself from. Identified regulation is dependent upon the duality of an internal desire for specific accomplishment, but the accomplishment is still being dictated by or measured against an external entity.

At the climax of the battle, with her old mentor Tissaia nearly falling to Nilfgaard, Yennefer receives the ultimate validation of her competence: Tissaia tells Yennefer that her legacy will be as the person who defeated Nilfgaard, if she can unleash all her

Chaos into a spell strong enough to destroy their army. Yennefer's external identified motivation to be regarded as the best sorcerer is proven correct. Her legacy will be created, even without having a child. She unleashes her Chaos using a fire spell. A magic that the Brotherhood has forbidden due to its volatility. With this dangerous magic at her disposal, Yennefer single-handedly wins the Battle of Sodden Hill. Then she loses her power.

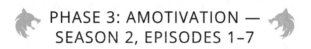

PHASE 3: AMOTIVATION —
SEASON 2, EPISODES 1–7

Without her magic, Yennefer loses her motivation and has to reexamine her core values.

A person who is experiencing amotivation has lost their desire to work toward achievement. Their lack of motivation could come from a lack of connection to an activity, or in Yennefer's case, a lack of belief in her own competence or not expecting to achieve the desired outcome from participation. After the Battle of Sodden Hill, Yennefer has no magic. For her entire life, her identity and motivation to do anything have come from one undeniable fact: Yennefer can do magic. With her power burned away, that is no longer true.

She is quickly captured first by Nilfgaard, then again by the elves Filavandrel and Francesca, and led to the extremely dangerous Voleth Meir. The treacherous witch is keenly aware of Yennefer's condition and needles Yennefer with her past motivations: First, the connection of a child that she cannot have. Second, her legacy as someone who had the competence to save the Brotherhood that hated her. And then the third: "Power, that's what you live for." For her entire life, Yennefer has lived for power. Either within the ranks of the Brotherhood or as a lone mage, Yennefer's life has been in pursuit of power and the autonomy it provides. Voleth Meir's observations are a complete list of the three key needs that SDT describes.

According to SDT, when a person's needs go unfulfilled, and that person cannot see a way to fulfill them, it becomes difficult to develop motivation, either external or internal. As a person becomes more unmotivated, factors like alienation and inauthenticity can begin to occur. In Yennefer's case, her alienation is not due to her capture by Nilfgaard, the elves, or Voleth Meir's taunting. Yennefer's identity as a magic-wielder has been the way she defines herself. Without her magic, she does not know who she is. This alienation makes her vulnerable.

Voleth Meir tells Yennefer that she has the power to return her magic, but she won't until Yennefer begs to have it back. After she escapes her captors and returns to the Brotherhood, Yennefer is welcomed back as the hero who defeated Nilfgaard. She starts to rebuild her basic needs as her sense of connection is rekindled. She feels valued as the person who saved the Brotherhood. However, just as when she was younger, she does not trust the Brotherhood. Yennefer learns that certain members believe that she cannot be trusted due to her time spent with Nilfgaardians after the Battle of Sodden Hill. To prove her loyalty, Yennefer agrees to execute a Nilfgaardian prisoner, the black knight Cahir. She has no magical power, and she is at the mercy of an organization that she cannot trust or influence. Yennefer eventually decides to flee the Brotherhood and bring Cahir with her to try and find a place in Nilfgaard.

AMOTIVATION

"You're born helpless so you find strength. Then that's all they want you for ... And you find power, and it turns to ash in your hands."

Yennefer's alienation is in flux. She wants to reconnect with the Brotherhood but doesn't trust them. They appear to value her skill as a mage, but she has hidden her lack of magic, therefore she cannot feel safe in her own sense

157

of competence. The only thing left to her is her sense of autonomy. Despite not having her magic, Yennefer's decision to disobey the Brotherhood and free Cahir shows that she is grasping at anything that can help her feel in control again. However, due to her fractured sense of identity, she does not know what to do next.

Yennefer and Cahir end up in Oxenfurt, where she is faced with continuing situations that she would normally be able to overcome easily with the use of her magic. As they flee the sewers, she screams at Cahir, "What's the fucking point? You're born helpless so you find strength. Then that's all they want you for, to use you. And you find love, but it isn't real. It's a wish someone made once before they even knew who you were. And you find power, and it turns to ash in your hands." Eventually the pair find Jaskir, who has been aiding elven refugees. After a tense reunion, Jaskir agrees to help Yennefer and Cahir escape Oxenfurt. However, Yennefer chooses not to escape the city, choosing instead to stay in town to help Jaskir.

For the first time in a very long time, Yennefer's sense of connectedness is growing. Why does she choose to stay behind and help Jaskir? It could be her need for connectedness. With her magic gone and her autonomy dwindling, she has no other choice but to feel empathy.

Desi and Ryan spent a considerable amount of time trying to understand the needs that everyone has for connection, competence, and autonomy. Their research tried to examine whether or not people satisfy their needs the same way over time. As simple as it may sound, they discovered people change the way they meet their needs as they experience different things. Yennefer's desire for her three key needs doesn't change, but the way she satisfies them does. During her time without magic, Yennefer is still trying to make connections with people, but unlike when she was a member of the Brotherhood or an independent, she isn't making connections out of a desire for power or status. She chooses to help Jaskir and the elves because she has experienced more at that point in her life than when she first joined the Brotherhood. Yennefer's amotivation is causing her to reevaluate the way she satisfies her needs.

When she eventually finds herself on the brink of regaining her magic, she agrees to help Voleth Meir by bringing her a child, Ciri. Yennefer's past dictates that a transactional relationship is how she can feel connected to people, so Voleth Meir's bargain makes sense. However, when Yennefer eventually discovers who Ciri is, she begins to doubt her decision.

Yennefer quickly discovers that Ciri's magical capabilities are tremendous, beyond even her own. During their escape from the Temple of Melitele, Yennefer does something she has never done before: she teaches. She decides that she needs to connect with Ciri and help her learn to control her Chaos.

At this point Yennefer's mission to deliver Ciri to Voleth Meir is at the front of her mind. Yennefer thinks she has returned to her old path of identified regulation, but she has doubts. During their journey together, Yennefer tells Ciri, "You can be too strong to fail or too weak to try," and "When you have power like this, never apologize." Yennefer's words come from her past experiences with the Brotherhood and the abusive way she was taught.

Yennefer's autonomy in this situation is in direct conflict with her competence and connectedness. Most of her life has been spent with her motivation coming from an external desire to be better than everyone around her. With her incredible magical skill, that goal was achievable. Now that her magic is broken, Yennefer is left with a choice: she can teach Ciri the same way that she learned, or break the cycle of abuse and betrayal that was so common with the Brotherhood. When she eventually chooses to be honest with Ciri, Yennefer believes she is giving up her magic forever. Her choice to be honest with Ciri demonstrates a decision to change the way she fulfills her needs based what she believes is right and not an external organization.

PHASE 4: INTRINSIC MOTIVATION — SEASON 2, EPISODE 8

Yennefer believes in herself and connects with others because she wants to.

Yennefer has decided that she is no longer interested in what power has to offer. She has cast aside the validation of the Brotherhood and Voleth Meir. Her motivation for a different way to connect with people has provided a new way for her to fulfill a key need. Yennefer wants to help Ciri because she believes it's the right thing to do. This choice is based on her internal morality. She knows that her experiences with the Brotherhood were transactional. She got power but she had to surrender her fertility. Yennefer knows how much people will want to manipulate or control Ciri due to her power. She knows the journey that Ciri could find herself on is painfully similar to her own.

Yennefer doesn't want anything from Ciri; she want wants to help her, not out of a desire to train the best student, or the most powerful wizard. Yennefer's desire is not transactional or based on anything external. In the hours before the final confrontation with Voleth Meir, Yennefer's intrinsic motivation becomes her primary motivation. She still has no magical power to speak of, but that doesn't stop her from being involved and trying to help Geralt free Ciri.

As the battle draws to its climax, Yennefer sacrifices herself to defeat Voleth Meir. This act of selflessness is a perfect representation that Yennefer is acting on what she considers to be the right

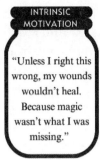

INTRINSIC MOTIVATION

"Unless I right this wrong, my wounds wouldn't heal. Because magic wasn't what I was missing."

thing to do. Much to her surprise, she doesn't die, and her magic is restored after Voleth Meir is defeated. With that victory, Yennefer is free from the witch's influence and also free from her old way of life.

She tells Geralt, "Unless I right this wrong, my wounds wouldn't heal. Because magic wasn't what I was missing." Yennefer could portal herself away and get back to her old life of acclaim and status, but she chooses to stay. Now that she has the chance to make her choices based on the core values that she has developed over a lifetime of experience, her motivations are her own. She can become the version of herself that she wants, regardless of how anyone measures her.

Yennefer has chosen to stay with Ciri and Geralt because she wants to, so her autonomy is intact. She has discovered that her competence isn't a reflection of her magical abilities. All of her skills and abilities can demonstrate her competence as a whole person. Finally, her sense of connection is fulfilled with her role as Ciri's teacher and Geralt's friend. She isn't using either of them to accomplish some hidden agenda, and neither of them is manipulating her. Her motivation to stay with them is intrinsic and comes from Yennefer's desire to do good for her friends and herself.

CONCLUSION

SDT is one of a myriad of ways to examine a character like Yennefer. Reflecting on the motivations that drive a character like her can provide people a chance to examine the motivations in their own lives. Are they seeking rewards for their actions? Are they ignoring one of their three key needs in favor of the others?

Have their life experiences given them a chance to recognize an opportunity to do something different and break a harmful cycle? Yennefer is not a perfect character, and her arrival at intrinsic motivation is neither perfect nor linear. Her end point is the result of many missteps and external influences, but even though she finds herself repeating her mistakes, she keeps moving. She meets new people, experiences new things and makes new choices. Eventually all three of her key needs are met to a degree when she can find herself free from a desire for external rewards and can rest in the contentment of knowing who she really is. Because destiny alone isn't sufficient.

About the Author

JOE LECONTE works in the substance use recovery office at Texas Christian University in the Counseling and Mental Health Center. He is a substance use counselor and peer support coordinator. He uses tabletop role-playing games in his weekly practice to help students dealing with loneliness and isolation. He is a Licensed Chemical Dependency Counselor and Licensed Professional Counselor – Associate in the state of Texas, under the supervision of Dr. Heather Shahan and Caroline Sahba.

References

Carton J. S. (1996). The differential effects of tangible rewards and praise on intrinsic motivation: A comparison of cognitive evaluation theory and operant theory. *The Behavior analyst, 19*(2), 237–255. https://doi.org/10.1007/BF03393167

Deci, E.L., Ryan, R.M. (2012) Self-Determination Theory. In P.A.M. Van Lange, A.W. Kruglanski & E. T. Higgins (Eds.), *Handbook of Theories of Social Psychology* (pp.416–437). SAGE Publications.

De Jong, P. & Berg, I.K. (2013) *Interviewing for Solutions* (4th ed.) Brooks/Cole CENGAGE Learning.

Hissrich, L.S. (Creator). (2019-Present) *The Witcher.* [TV Series]. Little Schmidt Productions, Hivemind, Platige Image, Netflix

Mullan, E., & Markland, D. (1997). Variations in self-determination across the stages of change for exercise in adults. *Motivation and Emotion, 21*(4), 349–362. https://doi-org.ezproxy.tcu.edu/10.1023/A:1024436423492

Patrick, H. Williams, G.C (2012) Self-determination theory: its application to health behavior and complementarity with motivational interviewing. *International Journal of Behavioral Nutrition and Physical Activity, 9* (18). https://doi.org/10.1186/1479-5868-9-18

Zamarripa, J., Castillo, I., Baños, R., Delgado, M., & Álvarez, O. (2018). Motivational Regulations Across the Stages of Change for Exercise in the General Population of Monterrey (Mexico). *Frontiers in psychology, 9*, 2368. https://doi.org/10.3389/fpsyg.2018.02368

9

YENNEFER'S FIGHT FOR FREEDOM IN THE WITCHER UNIVERSE: EXPLORING HER PATH THROUGH THE LENSES OF LIBERATION PSYCHOLOGIES

SYLWIA KORSAK

"It's not enough to possess Chaos. You and I, we must learn to control it. That is the essence of power. That is how we will move mountains. Together."

— Yennefer, *The Witcher, Season 3*

Yennefer of Vengerberg, a powerful sorceress of the fictional Witcherverse, journeys through it on her terms. She overcomes abuse, judgment, and systemic othering. Since the original books were published in the 1990s in Poland, her path has continued through the Polish editions of comic books, films, online games, English book translations and comic books, and finally, the Netflix series.

From a backstage figure serving *The Witcher*'s plot through many new interpretations, Yennefer grows into a leading independent and influential figure, inspiring women, feminists, and liberation practitioners. This essay explores Yennefer's journey through the lenses of liberation psychologies. It aims to inspire therapists working with displaced individuals to consider her as an example of healing from relational and systemic othering, resistance to it, and thriving.

Ignacio Martín-Baró and Paulo Freire, credited with initiating liberation psychology in the 1970s in Latin America, are rarely mentioned in the core therapeutic training. However, their work continued in many innovative psychological approaches globally, such as indigenous, art, feminist, queer, anti-oppressive, decolonizing, and climate crisis-aware therapies. Nowadays, Dr. Thema Bryant in the US, Taiwo Afuape in the UK, and many other practitioners worldwide promote liberation approaches within and outside psychology. The growing body of academic literature in English makes liberation psychologies more accessible. The Geek Therapeutics approach also opens opportunities to apply fundamental principles of liberation psychologies.

Unlike the Western and Euro-patriarchal approach to the word "liberation" (helping the oppressed), liberation psychologies support all parties involved in oppression. Practitioners offer support through critical analysis, new ways of individual and collective healing, and a new sense of common purpose. They focus on nurturing strengths, agency, and the capacity for critical thinking, feeling, and transformation. Practitioners critically review all aspects of their work, including the impact of psychological interventions on the client, thus refusing the myth of therapeutic neutrality.

Liberation therapists help clients re-author their lives (critically review and reshape their stories) to find new meaning in their experiences. They work with the client to map out their oppression landscape and contextualize those individual experiences. As a result, the clients start to understand that their mental health may be a healthy reaction to an unhealthy reality. Practitioners support clients' exploration of how power presents itself in their lives, including the perception of the therapist's power in the room. They normalize the client's responses, celebrate their resistance, and move toward bridging (affirmatively connecting with the perceived other), imagining new ways of being, and hopefully thriving.

Yennefer's journey through the Witcherverse is an example of successful liberation through re-authoring, critical awareness, and understanding of how power operates in her close relationships and her reality.

 ## RELATIONAL LIBERATION

Yennefer forms her closest relationships with Tissaia de Vries, Geralt of Rivia, and Cirilla of Cintra. Thanks to those relationships, she can heal from her traumatic childhood and claim her powerful position as a sorceress, lover, and mentor. Tissaia de Vries educates Yennefer in the Aretuza school for sorceresses, offering her emotional boundaries as well as education in magical skills and the Continent's politics. She provides a role model of an adoptive mother and a trusted female friend. With her guidance, Yennefer can re-author her social positioning from that of a disabled orphan to an influential sorceress. Geralt of Rivia invests his romantic feelings in a long-term, trusted relationship with Yennefer. He offers her unconditional respect and support in a world which doesn't value women. Even though the witcher and the sorceress are often tested by their individual trauma responses and external challenges, Yennefer can claim equal place and power in this partnership. Cirilla of Cintra arrives in Yennefer's life as

Geralt's Child of Surprise (a child destined to join him on his path) and eventually becomes Yennefer's adoptive daughter and apprentice of magic. In this relationship, we see Yennefer practicing critical awareness in passing her teachings to Cirilla. Those three relationships support Yennefer's journey of liberation.

 ## RE-AUTHORING WITH TISSAIA DE VRIES

Yennefer re-authors her early life through her relationship with Tissaia de Vries. Due to her kyphosis and mixed heritage (half-Elf), Yennefer experiences the trauma of severe bullying, neglect, physical and emotional abuse, and ultimate abandonment by her parents. Tissaia de Vries spots her magical powers and becomes her savior. She is a strict, authoritarian mentor (parent figure). In her early days at Aretuza boarding school for sorceresses, Yennefer struggles with feeling ugly, worthless, and lonely, which leads to a suicide attempt. Tissaia steps in and saves her life. In the books, she offers her beauty, while in the series, Yennefer claims beauty herself in exchange for fertility. Tissaia teaches her the balanced use of Chaos, which allows sorceresses to hold rare power in their society. Later in their relationship, she also offers mentoring and parenting advice on relationships and adult life. School is harsh, but it prepares Yennefer for their reality: power play, extreme violence, and abuse of women. When Yennefer continues living her adult life as a powerful and feared sorceress, Tissaia gradually switches to an equal relationship. She acknowledges and praises Yennefer's journey of re-authoring her life from an outcast orphan to a successful healer and community leader. She understands her need to have a child and admires her determination to resist the limitations of the sorcery world. Whether by choice (in the movies) or without (in the books), Yennefer has had to give up her fertility to become successful. However, by adopting and loving Cirilla, she re-authors herself to become a mother.

Re-authoring from the trauma of abuse requires support and the right conditions to nurture individual agency: a healing relationship, safety, remembrance and mourning, reconnection with ourselves, and commonality of our experience with others. The relationship with Tissaia offers Yennefer that. Tissaia, while admittedly a harsh teacher, maintains firm boundaries with her pupils. She teaches them how to move freely and successfully in a violent world of men. She holds Yennefer's hope in those darkest moments. She creates a contained space for Yennefer to process her grief and mourn her losses. She guides her toward her strengths as a new, empowered version of herself. Similarly, practitioners can use the therapeutic relationship to support identity work and recovery when working with displaced and abused clients.

EXPLORATION OF POWER WITH GERALT OF RIVIA

Yennefer continues her liberation by claiming equal power in romantic relationships. Her first relationship with Istredd at Aretuza prepares her for the complexities of love for Geralt. From the first Polish comic book presenting Geralt's teen years, we learn he also had a young love, Aideen. The initial meeting of the sorceress and the witcher, especially in the books, signals the nature of their future relationship: mutual healing from traumatic childhoods, strong temperaments, and deep love bridging divides. Yennefer knows Geralt's story of childhood mutations and grief for lost childhood friends. Looking into her eyes, Geralt sees a glimpse of Yennefer's childhood and decides to commit to her. Their differences set them apart, yet they find healing in similarities. Yennefer loves glamour and power, while Geralt avoids fashionable courts. She is versed in people skills and strategizing, while Geralt is impulsive, reactive, and disorganized. They are both strong-willed, feared but respected rebels. Through a series of encounters and their shared love for Cirilla, they work through their trauma responses and, ultimately, form a deep bond. They reenact a lot of internalized oppression by hurting, abandoning, betraying, and pushing each other away. However, they gradually find a way back to each other. Yennefer finds home and belonging as an equal in this relationship.

We see Yennefer's exploration of power in this relationship. She is an unusual woman for her times: independent, outspoken, and influential; openly angry, vengeful, and feared, but also successful. She bosses men around, including Geralt. For example, she rushes him out of the bath in the *Witcher* game. In Bielanin's story (in a unique Ukrainian-Russian collection), she asks the witcher to take the rubbish out. Additionally, her sexuality represents power. Yennefer is in charge of her sexuality and expects others to respect it. In the "Curse of Crows" comic, she punishes Geralt for ignoring her needs by sending him on an unnecessary quest. In the opening of *The Witcher 3: Wild Hunt*, Geralt has to wait for her to kiss him. In the movie, she asks him to kiss her during the Conclave Ball. It's radical to see a woman receive such respect, initiate sex, and practice consent in such a violent, patriarchal universe.

Practitioners can use their relationship creatively in therapy to highlight the complexities of power and consent using the Power Threat Meaning Framework. This framework maps out how power operates in people's lives, what threats it presents, and what meaning they make of it. When done with the client's active participation, a therapist can model change through healthy resistance and critical awareness of how power operates in their lives and affects their well-being.

CRITICAL AWARENESS THROUGH CIRILLA OF CINTRA

Yennefer passes on the legacy of her liberation to the next generation of women by raising Cirilla's critical awareness of power and womanhood. Cirilla of Cintra is the witcher's adoptive child with the unique powers of the Elder Blood. When Geralt realizes his limitations in magical skills, he asks Yennefer to train the child. This becomes a fantastic opportunity for the sorceress to become an adoptive mother. Initially, their relationship feels stormy. Cirilla is wild, independent, and distrustful. After a steady royal upbringing, she experiences severe trauma and PTSD, so Yennefer resorts to authoritative parenting. She teaches the girl the basics of magic and femininity in their patriarchal world. She educates Cirilla on the consequences of her actions and the burden of responsibility for her unique talents. She prepares her for life in a violent world where power may claim Cirilla's title, body, or even life. They don't always get along. In the movie, Yennefer loses her powers during the Battle of Sodden Hill. She then almost betrays Cirilla and Geralt in a desperate search for an infertility cure. She evaluates her options and decides to invest love, trust, and the rest of her life in the girl, as she realizes that Cirilla is her only chance to become a mother. She shows humility and works hard to regain Geralt's and the girl's trust. Cirilla also rebels against Yennefer, only to mature into deep feelings of gratitude and love, thanks to her steady early upbringing. Ultimately, the two women work through their mistakes and bond over their love for Geralt, gradually forming a trusted mother-daughter relationship. As Cirilla matures, Yennefer becomes her fierce protector. She advocates for her safety so much that she is willing to fight for the Continent's peace and unite all mages and nations to keep her adoptive daughter safe. Cirilla, in return, offers her adoptive parents safe passage to the other world (in the books).

Therapists can explore Yennefer's role in raising Cirilla's critical awareness by applying the model of racial recovery, which comprises acknowledging traumas, sharing experiences, exploring safety and self-care while grieving the losses, exploring shame and internalized oppression, exploring anger, and finally learning healthy coping and resistance. Yennefer wisely holds Cirilla through all those stages of liberation, raising an independent and powerful woman. When working with displaced clients, holding space for their realizations of life's limitations is vital. Practitioners need to consider the cost of risky events and environments. Only from this place clients can start recovery toward healthier futures.

 ## INDIVIDUAL JOURNEY

Yennefer's life journey and significant relationships inform her liberation. However, reflecting on her individual path from displacement to empowerment can help identify ways therapists can support the client's unique experiences. Yennefer re-authors her life by embracing her shadow, healing, and fighting for a better life. She understands gender discrimination, making her mark on the Continent. She adopts a healthy resistance to the challenges of her reality, carving a new path for herself.

 EMBRACING HER SHADOW FOR RE-AUTHORING

The crucial ingredient of Yennefer's success is her ability to embrace the possibility of change. Arriving at Aretuza is terrifying. However, she faces her challenges and learns to use her strengths. She realizes the unique benefits of her profession, such as beauty, influential social positioning, and incredible magical skills. Yennefer acknowledges that this is her opportunity to become a powerful woman. That power is signaled in the language of the universe; for instance, Geralt's title, "The Witcher," is a female version of this profession ("witch+er"). Yennefer becomes an independent, respected sorceress. Her friendship with Tissaia and love for Geralt and Cirilla help her heal from childhood trauma. However, it is Yennefer alone who fights to maintain her freedoms and privileges. She continues facing judgment and violence, but thanks to her personal agency, she can successfully move through the Witcherverse.

For clients recovering from abuse, war, and other forms of violence, therapists can offer safe spaces and relationships to embrace the cost of risky events and environments. Liberation psychology proposes assisting clients in acknowledging their wounding, supporting their historical memory of trauma safely, and supporting their critical reflection. Those conditions allow displaced clients to process their losses and move forward to creative re-authoring of their identity. Clients can move from fatalism toward critical consciousness with agency and the power to perform roles differently for their well-being.

 EXPLORING GENDER POWER IMBALANCE

Yennefer becomes a powerful sorceress in a patriarchal world. She practices embodied activism using fashion, spatial positioning, and language to signal power. She travels elegantly dressed in black and white garments, flattering her beauty and stressing her powers. She celebrates her emotions. In the series, during the Conclave Ball, she places her neck-decorating star, unusually, above her heart to announce her love for Geralt. She dutifully learns to manage the Chaos but also studies power over people. Yennefer becomes an effective, strategic leader outside and inside her community. She refuses to embrace the attributes prescribed to women by the brutal patriarchal society, such as dependency, submissiveness, politeness, and lack of sexual agency. It is patriarchy that forces sorceresses to get involved in politics. Yennefer becomes a strong, powerful, but also independent sorceress. She refuses to serve her king. She fights for her equal rights, expecting her universe to accommodate all her needs.

Yennefer models high awareness of her internalized oppression and a strong, healthy resistance to it. Therapists can work with displaced clients to identify the impact of power on their experiences. In liberation psychology, this awareness is a basic condition for the oppressed to "find the oppressor out," (Freire, 2017). Practitioners may need to educate their clients on alternative ways of operating in society, such as refusing a hierarchical approach to power and owning "power as-it-is" (power belonging to everyone, Salami, 2023). When clients realize their oppression, they can start to invite creativity, hope, inspiration, play, and futurism into the healing process.

HEALTHY RESISTANCE TO UNHEALTHY REALITY

In the violent, patriarchal reality of the Witcherverse, Yennefer often finds herself in situations and communities full of paradoxes that women still face today. In the books, her reputation is negative because of the very characteristics and behaviors attributed to men: being strong, opinionated, and fierce. She's faced with impossible choices. In the movie, when asked to kill Cahir (a Nilfgaardian soldier) to prove her loyalty to the mages, she risks becoming a murderer. Yennefer is well aware that this public execution would make her a criminal, so she decides to spare Cahir's life, escape, and clear her name. She carries the legacy of her childhood anxious attachment but also practices resistance: she is often abrupt and openly outspoken about the injustices of her life. In the movie, especially upon her return to Aretuza, Yennefer names the cruelty of her training and disagrees with powerful men's use of female sorceresses in the political scene. Across all genres, she calls out the situation of women in the Witcherverse, famously cursing so much that it makes men blush.

It can be liberating for displaced clients to allow themselves a safe space for anger and healthy resistance. Therapists can help them process those complex emotions healthily. "Understanding the therapeutic significance of resistance is important because while the workings of power are often invisible, resistance is generally more evident," (Afuape, 2012). Professional acknowledgment of the harm done, and validation of a healthy response to it, can be the first step on a journey toward the client's authentic and integrated self. This also includes taking a step back and reflecting on the practitioner's role in therapy—exploring all possible collusion points with the oppressive systems. For example, Freud himself had to change his initial theories from thoughts supporting women's experiences of harm to the need for healing female psychosis (mental illness). He realized that his fellow male academics wouldn't accept women's valid stories of harm. Contemporary reconciliation work finally enters the world of psychology. Therefore, therapists can support clients better with access to those new perspectives.

 ## YENNEFER'S EMERGENCE IN THE WITCHERVERSE

Yennefer's relational and individual liberation continues beyond the original Polish books, films, and comics through English comic books, movies, online games, board games, and a recent cookbook. The sorceress becomes an archetype of a strong, independent, powerful woman. Each new interpretation of Yennefer's character unfolds a richer story, allowing increasingly more space for her voice in the Witcherverse. It may be tempting to assume that *The Witcher*'s violent, hateful universe is fictional. However, not only does it reflect the reality of women during the twelfth century, it also announces the horrific witch hunts that, in some shape and form, continue until this day. This wider lens is critical to how therapists can use Yennefer's archetype for liberation work with displaced clients. Liberation psychology refuses to stay neutral to the systems therapists operate in—systems that may cause harm and distress. Thus, exploring the emergence of Yennefer's voice in Poland, in the English-speaking world, and globally is helpful.

YENNEFER'S JOURNEY AND IMPORTANCE IN POLAND

The original Polish books contain minimal mentions of Yennefer's story. She appears in them for the purpose of Geralt's plot. In the '90s, the *Witcher* books gained loyal fans in Poland, so the first comic books by Polch and Parowski (in Polish) soon followed. They articulate Yennefer's (and Geralt's) first visual expressions but only develop Geralt's childhood story. Yennefer's insignificance coincides with the fading of women's rights in Poland. While Sapkowski's universe is fundamental in re-authoring Slavic mythology (the original source of vampires and werewolves) globally, it focuses on patriarchal masculinity. It paints the world of the male god Perun, not that of the original Slavic Great Goddess. The books are packed with sexism and sexual, verbal, and domestic abuse of women. Thus, signposting survivors of sexual abuse to them requires a lot of caution. Very few female characters escape discrimination and harm in the original books, and Polish comic books still depict female characters with very few garments on them.

The Witcher video games by CD Projekt Red promote the universe globally. In *The Witcher 3: Wild Hunt* (2015), Yennefer returns. In the game companion book, she narrates an entire chapter about magic. The new comic books published by Dark Horse Comics in English start to introduce female artists and feminist themes. In 2014 and 2016, Trickster, the Polish Research Society for Pop Culture and Pop Culture Education, published two e-books on the psychology of *The Witcher*. They include studies of female representation, the role of witches, and othering in this universe. Gradually, as the resistance of the Women's Black March of 2016 marked the beginning of the fight for women's rights in

Poland, Yennefer emerges stronger and more vocal in her consequent interpretations, too.

In 2019, the Netflix series launched. Lauren Schmidt Hissrich, the female producer and screenwriter, collaborated with Polish artists and Sapkowski. Yennefer returns with a fully developed story, equally important to that of Geralt and Cirilla. The sorceress loudly calls out discrimination against women and other forms of injustice on the Continent, while in Poland, the women's fight for rights continued. In 2021, a Polish sex therapist and podcaster Marta Niedźwiecka dedicated an episode of her show to Yennefer and her role in women's liberation. All-Poland Women's Strikes continued, calling for female participation in politics and fighting for women's and LGBTQIA+ rights. Yennefer fell victim to the irritated Polish patriarchy once again. In Ostrołęka, a local politician complained about a youth council initiative which allowed an oak tree to be named after Yennefer. He claimed it offended the Polish word "oak" (which in Polish is masculine) in an attempt to mock the progressive, gender-affirming politics.

In the autumn of 2023, Yennefer came back in time to celebrate the victory of Polish activists. The day before the general elections, psychologist Agnieszka Kramm explored Yennefer's archetype as a symbol of feminism in the Polish mainstream press. Kramm reminded women to vote. The following day, Poland witnessed a record participation of women in elections and a significant increase of female politicians in parliament as a result. The elections brought back the liberal opposition, announcing significant policies supporting health and other basic human rights for women and the LGBTQIA+ community. Thirty percent of parliament members were women. The female 30 percent of the Council of Ministers were now called "ministera/ministerka" (female version of "minister"). Two Polish female authors, Anita Sarna and Karolina Krupecka, culminated seven years of their research and published *The Witcher Cookbook*. It features a female book narrator, a photo of lilac and gooseberries (Yennefer's perfume) next to the first recipe, and Geralt's omelet for Yennefer. CD Projekt RED ran a successful crowdfunding for a new Witcher-themed board game featuring Yennefer as one of its characters. From a supporting role in the plot, Yennefer became a significant character in the Witcherverse.

Liberation therapists must consider their past, current, and future realities. Practitioners can tap into Yennefer's journey for ideas and inspiration to support displaced women. Many liberation therapists operate outside of traditional psychology spaces, collaborating with other professionals and supporting healing through many mediums. While the 2007 release of the first online Witcher game played a key role in promoting this universe worldwide, the 2015 *The Witcher 3: Wild Hunt* brought Yennefer to the centre of it. It inspired Polish psychologists and sociologists to start exploring the impact of her character in the representation of women's rights. Yennefer may play an important role in the therapy room in supporting healing from gender-based violence. Given recent changes in her homeland, it is safe to assume that this archetype's voice is only warming up.

YENNEFER IN THE ENGLISH-SPEAKING WORLD

Since 2007, the popularity of the *Witcher* games and strong fandom advocacy led to the translations of the original books into English. The books contain many English references. Yennefer's name resonates with Gwenevere, the legendary Queen of England (also King Arthur's wife). Yennefer's adventures contain hints of the witch hunts. Geralt's party encounters a priest accusing an innocent girl of witchcraft. At the end of the saga, Yennefer hears direct warnings that the time of sorcery will soon be over. It's chilling to think about the millions of people, predominantly women, who lost their property and lives to the witch hunts emerging in Europe in the fourteenth century. During the witch hunts, women lost their last remaining spaces and roles of power. In the fifteenth century, women were banned from brewing and selling ale. The prosecution of female healers led to men taking over medical duties. Gender-based prosecutions built up gradually and spread to the US as well. The inclusion of child witnesses in the UK Pendle trials formalized law about the valid use of child witnesses, which later impacted the lives of women elsewhere, for example, in the Salem trials. Systemic targeting of female sexuality and infertility, seizing their property, and developing a legal system targeting all women destroyed the fabric of female communities. Isolated from each other, scared of their own beauty, and internalizing their own oppression, women continue living in a world ruled by patriarchy. In a world where women remain on trial to this day, Yennefer's archetype offers them hope for a more equitable, empowering future.

The witch archetype becomes strongly associated with the fight for female liberation. From the fight for voting rights to the recent #MeToo movement (initiated by Tarana Burke and reaching the therapy profession as well) and the rise of modern witchcraft as a fashion statement (such as the Chaos Magic trend), artistic expression, or lifestyle, Yennefer has become a much-needed archetype. "As well as a conduit for pain, defiance and female power, the witch is also a healing figure," (Toon, 2021). The witch archetype models resistance to unbearable circumstances, pride in beauty and strength, and hopefulness in times of despair. All those aspects can be utilized in support of displaced clients. Yennefer's freedom reminds us that the power of healing does not strictly belong to the trained medical professional. As Dr. Thema Bryant reminds us: "We forget that psychology doesn't hold a monopoly on healing."

YENNEFER AND THE GLOBAL MAJORITY

Yennefer's complex personality crosses the traditional divide between good and bad magic. The stories of bad and good witches appear all around the world. In many cultures, the judgment about a witch's good or bad intentions is linked to her social status. As in *The Witcher*, official healers are uplifted (mages, sorceresses), whereas informal healers are prosecuted (witches). With the spread of the Western idea of development, healing itself has become institutionalized in many cultures. As a result, institutional, state-funded therapy can cause harm and target disempowered groups.

Yennefer's rebel archetype emerges in the context of the recent decolonizing trends in psychology. With the rise of healthy resistance of disempowered groups, stories of female healers emerge once again. In new versions of global witch stories, witches are praised for the hopefulness, courage, and the richness of their healing wisdom. In light of the global climate crisis, the integration of all methods of healing and all cultures becomes a priority. The newly remembered acceptance of humankind's complexity, fluidity, and diversity bridges Western psychology with the richness of healing practiced by the Global Majority across all continents.

Liberation psychologies operate beyond the anti-oppressive and decolonizing practices. Liberation practitioners aim to create local, collective, nurturing spaces for restoration, healing, and thriving. The themes of othering and displacement are universal, but the solutions required to address them are unique to each community. Applying Western, Euro-patriarchal healing methods may not support liberation for all. As Martín-Baró's friend, liberation practitioner Ignacio Dobles states: "I don't think it's about transporting categories from one place to another. I think it is about thinking together and working together on the problems with the collaboration perspective and putting problems first." When working with displaced clients, therapists have an ethical responsibility to support the client respectfully, creatively, and flexibly, prioritizing their culture.

 CONCLUSION

Yennefer's journey of liberation suggests the possibility of a better world for all. Violence and misuse of power thrive on the isolation of individuals and groups. Maybe if displaced clients embrace the archetype of the witch—her agency to resist judgment and create new stories, critical awareness of Chaos and how power operates— they can find new ways to heal. With the new *Witcher* book, the new movie series, and a new edition of the board game expected in 2024, it may be helpful to pause and reflect on how Yennefer's character can help us all liberate ourselves from life's limitations. We need to imagine new possibilities. Reinventing our ways opens up cracks for healing from the impact of dysfunctional systems.

We can tap into geek culture archetypes to support that healing process. If Geralt's character can teach students psychology, maybe Yennefer can teach practitioners, too. Of course, every person's individual interpretation of her archetype may be unique. One person's Yennefer may walk out of an abusive home barefoot with her baby in her arms, courageously asking a kind neighbor for help. Another person's Yennefer may hesitate, but with trust and validation could collect the courage to share his story of a torturous boarding school. Meanwhile, someone else's

Yennefer may remain still and quiet in anticipation, aware of their risky reality, waiting for the time when not only gaming companies will change their logos to the Pride flag. Their Yennefer may be hopeful, knowing that this time is already unfolding. Everyone's Yennefer matters. That is where humankind's richness and real power lie: in the hope of new stories.

Acknowledgments and Positioning

Land acknowledgment: To the Dobunni people of Bristol, UK.

Author's identities: nondisabled, cisgender, female-identifying, White, Polish with British citizenship; integrated counselor supporting survivors of sexual abuse, other complex trauma and digital well-being challenges, working online, in VR and Nature.

Context: In Poland, the rights of women and the LGBTQIA+ community have been suppressed and threatened in recent years. In autumn 2023, the liberal opposition was elected with a significant increase in female participation in the political process. The UK is experiencing the post-Brexit reality and increasingly hostile environment and policies. Globally, we are facing economic instability, multiple instances of genocide, war, and breach of human rights, COVID+ reality, and climate crisis.

Gratitude: Thank you to Dr. Anthony Bean and all Geek Therapeutics colleagues, the Voxel Hub Advisory Board, Jamillah Knowles and Dan. I thank all past and present liberation practitioners and healers. My heart goes to all the women and people of all genders who have lost lives and continue suffering abuse and discrimination. My special gratitude goes to Ildikó for showing me the true power of Sisterhood.

About the Author

SYLWIA KORSAK (SHE/HER) is a liberation practitioner working with a wide range of approaches centered around the client's safety, diversity, and agency. She is a qualified integrated counselor and coach. Sylwia has training and over two decades of experience in education, coaching, digital marketing, social and charity work, online activism, business ethics, and digital well-being. She grew up in Poland, studied in Hungary, and worked around the world before settling in the UK over a decade ago. She is the founder of VoxelHub.org, a private practice that delivers consultancy, coaching, and counseling for digital well-being and liberation. In the therapeutic setting, Sylwia has experience offering grief, complex psychological needs, trauma, PTSD, addiction, anxiety and depression support. She supports clients experiencing displacement, such as the LGBTQIA+ community, neurodiverse clients and clients from various multicultural backgrounds. She is a passionate geek and loves working online and in Virtual Reality, as well as outdoors, reconnecting clients with nature. Additionally, she is supporting survivors of sexual abuse through the Kinergy Bristol service. She offers CPD training in liberation psychology, VR therapies and digital well-being at the Iron Mill College of Counselling in Exeter, UK.

References

Afuape, T. (2012) Power, Resistance and Liberation in Therapy with Survivors of Trauma: To Have Our Hearts Broken (1st ed). Routledge.

Akomolafe, B. (2017) These Wilds Beyond Our Fences: Letters to My Daughter on Humanity's Search for Home. North Atlantic Books.

Bates, L. (2020) Men who hate women. Simon and Shuster.

Bates, L. (2023) Fix the System, Not the Women. Simon and Shuster.

Batylda, M. (2015) The World of the Witcher. Video Game Compendium. Dark Horse Books.

Bean, A.M. (2018) Working with Video Gamers and Games in Therapy: A Clinician's Guide(1st ed.) Routledge.

Bean, A.M., Daniel Jr., E.S & Hays, S.A. (2020) Integrating Geek Culture Into Therapeutic Practice: The Clinician's Guide To Geek Therapy. Leyline Publishing.

Boyle, M. & Johnstone, L. (2018) A Straight Talking Introduction to the Power Threat Meaning Framework. An Alternative to Psychiatric Diagnosis. PCCS Books Ltd.

Brooks, L. (2021, March 8) Why Did Women Stop Dominating the Beer Industry? Smithsonian Magazine. https://www.smithsonianmag.com/history/women-used-dominate-beer-industry-until-witch-accusations-started-pouring-180977171/

Bryant, T. PhD (2022) Homecoming: Overcome Fear and Trauma to Reclaim Your Whole, Authentic Self. Tarcher Perigee.

Bryant, T. PhD (2023) New Views on Mental Health—Day 1. *Mental Health Global Summit 2023*. https://www.mentalhealthglobalsummit.com/schedule/

Bryant, T. PhD & Ocampo, C. (2008) A Therapeutic Approach to the Treatment of Racist-Incident-Based Trauma. https://doi.org/10.1300/J135v06n04_01

Burke, T. (2021) Unbound: My Story of Liberation and the Birth of the Me Too Movement (1st ed.). Headline Book Publishing.

Charney, N. & Slapšak, S. (2023) The Slavic Myths (1st ed.) Thames and Hudson Ltd.

CD Projekt Red (2015, April 17) The Witcher 3: Wild Hunt on Xbox One available for pre-order from Xbox Games Store. *The Witcher News*. https://www.thewitcher.com/gb/en/news/1006/the-witcher-3-wild-hunt-on-xbox-one-available-for-pre-order-from-xbox-games-store

CD Projekt Red (2021, June 16) Pride Month charity stream is coming! *The Witcher News*. https://www.thewitcher.com/gb/en/news/38597/pride-month-charity-stream-is-coming

CD Projekt Red (2023, September 12) New board game is coming—The Witcher: Path of Destiny! *The Witcher News*. https://www.thewitcher.com/us/en/news/48895/new-board-game-is-coming-the-witcher-path-of-destiny

Chollet, M. (2022) In Defense of Witches: Why women are still on trial. St. Martin's Press.

Connellan, S. (2023, July 3) 'The Witcher' Season 3's ball costumes are packed with hidden clues. *Mashable TV Shows*. https://mashable.com/article/the-witcher-ball-season-3-costumes-clues-lucinda-wright

Drewniak, P. (2016) Are we there yet? A snapshot in the haphazard history of Wiedźmin's English translations. In Dudziński, R. & Płoszaj.J. (Eds.) Wiedźmin – polski fenomen popkultury [The Witcher—Polish Pop Culture Phenomenon]. Trickster. http://tricksterzy.pl/wiedzmin-polski-fenomen-popkultury-w-biblioteczce-trickstera/.

Dudziński, R. & Płoszaj. J. (2016) Wiedźmin – polski fenomen popkultury [The Witcher—Polish Pop Culture Phenomenon]. Trickster. OER Commons. Retrieved January 6, 2024, from http://tricksterzy.pl/wiedzmin-polski-fenomen-popkultury-w-biblioteczce-trickstera/.

Edwards, E. (2021) The Witcher Season 1 timeline explained: How the Netflix show's storylines fit together. *Gamesradar*. https://www.gamesradar.com/the-witcher-netflix-timeline-yennefer-geralt-ciri/

Federici, S. (2021) Caliban and the Witch: Women, the Body and Primitive Accumulation (1st ed.). Penguin Classics.

Flamma, A. (2016) Postaci kobiet w grze Wiedźmin – znaczenie i analiza [Female characters in the Witcher game—meaning and analysis]. In Dudziński, R. & Płoszaj.J. (Eds.) Wiedźmin – polski fenomen popkultury [The Witcher—Polish Pop Culture Phenomenon]. Trickster. http://tricksterzy.pl/wiedzmin-polski-fenomen-popkultury-w-biblioteczce-trickstera/.

Frazer-Caroll, M. (2023) Mad World: The Politics of Mental Health. Pluto Press.

Free Documentary—History (2021, February 5). The Gruesome Trial of the Pendle Hill Witches. [Video]. YouTube. https://www.youtube.com/watch?v=my5cm6tfTz8

Freire, P. (2017) Pedagogy of the Oppressed (13th ed). Penguin Classics.

Gibson, M. (2013) Witchcraft: A History in Thirteen Trials. Simon & Schuster.

Godzinski, B. (2021, July 29) W Polsce jak w lesie. Radny PiS rozsierdzony, bo dąb dostał żeńskie imię czarodziejki z „Wiedźmina" [In Poland like in the woods. PiS politician angry that an oak was named after a Witcher sorceress]. *SpidersWeb Rozrywka*. https://rozrywka.spidersweb.pl/wiedzmin-drzewa-ostroleka-radny-pis

Hawkins, P. & Ryde. J. (2019) Integrative Psychotherapy in Theory and Practice: A Relational, Systemic and Ecological Approach. Jessica Kingsley Publishers

Herman, J. (1994) Trauma and Recovery: From Domestic Abuse to Political Terror. Rivers Oram Press/Pandora List.

Husain, S. (1993) The Virago Book of Witches. Virago Press.

James, J., Matthews, C. & Matthews J. (2015) The Fourth Gwenevere. Jo Fletcher Books.

Johnson, R. PhD. (2023) Embodied Activism: Engaging the Body to Cultivate Liberation, Justice, and Authentic Connection- A Practical Guide for Transformative Social Change. North Atlantic Books.

Kilmer, J. PhD & Kilmer, E. Phd (2023) Resilience and Trauma. Ciri Fiona Riannon. In Kowert, R. (Ed.), The Psychgeist of Pop Culture: The Witcher. ETC Press.

Krzywicka, E. (2016) Śladami Białego Wilka. O ukraińsko-rosyjskich Opowieściach ze świata wiedźmina [In the Witcher's footsteps. On Ukrainian-Russian Tales from the Witcher Universe]. In Dudziński, R. & Płoszaj. J. (Eds.) (2016) Wiedźmin – polski fenomen popkultury [The Witcher—Polish Pop Culture Phenomenon]. Trickster. http://tricksterzy.pl/wiedzmin-polski-fenomen-popkultury-w-biblioteczce-trickstera/.

Lee, A.D. & Palmer, M. (2020) #MeToo—counsellors and psychotherapists speak about sexual violence and abuse. PCCS Books.

Martín-Baró, I. (1996) Writings for a Liberation Psychology: Written by Ignacio Martín-Baró. Harvard University Press.

Matuszek, D. (2016) Koniec męskości, albo Wiedźmina opisanie [The End of Masculinity, or a Sketch of the Witcher]. In Śląskie Studia Polonistyczne [Silesian Polish Linguistic Studies] volume 1–2, 185–200, https://core.ac.uk/download/pdf/197753114.pdf .

Mhalfy1 (2022, March 26) Ignacio Dobles on Liberation Psychology. [Video]. YouTube. https://www.youtube.com/watch?v=-OoLJ8YCLo8 .

Mullan, J. (2023) Decolonizing Therapy: Oppression, Historical Trauma, and Politicizing Your Practice. WW Norton & Co.

Niedźwiecka, M. (Host) (2021) *O Zmierzchu Podcast.* [Audio podcast episode] Po co nam czarodziejki? Spytajmy Yennefer i Ciri [Why do we need sorceresses? Let's ask Yennefer and Ciri]. https://podcasts.apple.com/gb/podcast/s03e52-po-co-nam-czarodziejki-spytajmy-yennefer-i-ciri/id1465709276?i=1000546087578 .

Olekszyk. J. (2023, September 12) Postać czarownicy wraca. Kobiety odzyskują głos! [The witch character is back. Sorceresses regain their voice!] *Zwierciadło.* https://zwierciadlo.pl/psychologia/522150,1,kobiety-odzyskuja-moc--postac-czarownicy-wraca.read .

Polch, B., Sapkowski, A. & Parowski, M. (2022) Wiedźmin [The Witcher]. Prószyński Media.

Pitt Rivers Museum (2023) Marina Abramović @ Pitt Rivers Museum. https://www.prm.ox.ac.uk/marina-abramovic-pitt-rivers-museum .

Robert Dudziński, R., Flamma, A., Kowalczyk,K. & Płoszaj, J (2015) Wiedźmin – bohater masowej wyobraźni [The Witcher—the hero of mass imagination]. Trickster. OER Commons. Retrieved January 6, 2024, from http://tricksterzy.pl/nowy-tom-tricksterawiedzmin-bohater-masowej-wyobrazni/ .

Salami, M. (2023) Sensuous Knowledge: A Black Feminist Approach for Everyone. Bloomsbury Academic.

Sapkowski, A. (2013) Sezon Burz [Season of Storms]. Niezależna Oficyna Wydawnicza Nowa Sapkowski, A. (2014) Ostatnie Życzenie [The Last Wish]. Niezależna Oficyna Wydawnicza Nowa

Sapkowski, A. (2014) Miecz Przeznaczenia [Sword of Destiny]. Niezależna Oficyna Wydawnicza Nowa.

Sapkowski, A. (2014) Krew Elfów [Blood of Elves]. Niezależna Oficyna Wydawnicza Nowa.

Sapkowski, A. (2014) Czas Pogardy [Time of Contempt] Niezależna Oficyna Wydawnicza Nowa.

Sapkowski, A. (2014) Chrzest Ognia [Baptism of Fire]. Niezależna Oficyna Wydawnicza Nowa.

Sapkowski, A. (2014) Wierza Jaskółki [The Tower of the Swallow]. Niezależna Oficyna. Wydawnicza Nowa.

Sapkowski, A. (2014) Pani Jeziora [The Lady of The Lake] Niezależna Oficyna Wydawnicza Nowa.

Sarna, A. & Krupecka, K. (2023) The Witcher Official Cookbook. Gollancz.

Sedgwick, I. (2023) Rebel Folklore. DK.

Shanley, M. (2023) Psychology of Attachment. Yennefer of Vengerberg. In Kowert, R. (Ed.), The Psychgeist of Pop Culture: The Witcher. ETC Press.

Sztybor, B., Motyka, A. Strychowska, M. Mir, A. & Del Rey, V. R. (2023) The Witcher Omnibus. Dark Horse Books.

Tobin, P., Querio, J., Kowalski, P. & Bertoloni, M. (2020) The Witcher Omnibus 2. Dark Horse Books.

Toon, F. (2021) 'We are the granddaughters of the witches you couldn't burn.' Penguin Features. https://www.penguin.co.uk/articles/2021/03/francine-toon-pine-inner-witch-violence-against-women .

Ucherek, D. (2016) Czarodziejki (i czarodzieje) w świecie wiedźmina [Femal (and Male) Sorceresses in the Witcher universe.] In Dudziński, R. & Płoszaj.J. (Eds.) Wiedźmin – polski fenomen popkultury [The Witcher—Polish Pop Culture Phenomenon]. Trickster. http://tricksterzy.pl/wiedzmin-polski-fenomen-popkultury-w-biblioteczce-trickstera/.

Uniwersytet Śląski [University of Silesia] (2022, March 26) Czy Wiedźmin utopiłby Marzannę? Psychologia na tropie fantastycznej zagadki [Would Witcher drown Morana, goddess of winter? Psychology investigating fantastic mystery] [Video]. YouTube. https://www.youtube.com/watch?v=XHWLx .

Watkins, M. & Shulman, H. (2008) Toward Psychologies of Liberation (Critical Theory and Practice in Psychology and the Human Sciences). Basingstoke: Palgrave Macmillan

Yotka, S. (2015) Is Fashion Entering a Year of Magical Thinking? A Conversation With Pop Culture's Favorite Trend Forecasters. Vogue. https://www.vogue.com/article/k-hole-magic-trend-report

10

SEXUAL AND RELATIONSHIP ORIENTATIONS IN *THE WITCHER*

WENDI "NICKI" LINE

"You've mistaken the stars reflected on the surface of the lake at night for the heavens."

— Mystical voice speaking to Ciri, *Blood of Elves*

 ## SEXUAL AND RELATIONSHIP ORIENTATIONS IN *THE WITCHER*

In recent years, the portrayal of queer characters and alternative relationship orientations in the media has gained significant attention and importance. Much of the visibility and community recognition surrounding these themes stem from their portrayal in various forms of media such as film, television, and literature. Works like *The Witcher* offer a platform for the exploration of diverse sexual and relationship orientations, contributing to a broader understanding and acceptance of LGBTQIA+, ENM (Ethical Nonmonogamy), and power exchange communities. This surge in representation can be attributed to several factors, including the growing number of individuals openly identifying as queer, the evolving definitions of gender identity, and improved methods for accounting for minority populations in demographic surveys.

Similarly, awareness of and identification with nonmonogamous relationships has risen over the past decade, although such relationships are not explicitly recorded in census data. Moreover, social scientific and sociological research on power exchange communities has seen exponential growth over the last forty years. Within *The Witcher*'s extensive universe, a multitude of characters embody various sexual and relationship orientations, offering nuanced portrayals and exploring the complexities that may arise. From prominent figures like Ciri and Jaskier to supporting characters like Prince Radovid and Philippa Eilhart, the series provides a rich tapestry of LGBTQIA+ representation. Furthermore, characters like Geralt and Philippa navigate intricate webs of relationships, including ENM dynamics and power exchanges, without these aspects dominating the central plotlines. This subtlety allows for a normalization of diverse relationships and creates space for exploration and dialogue. As Staci Newmahr notes, science-fiction and fantasy literature often embrace alternative sexualities, fostering open attitudes toward desire and relationship autonomy. In light of this, this chapter aims to explore the representations of LGBTQ+, ENM, and BDSM within the Witcherverse.

 ## QUEER REPRESENTATION

In the intricate tapestry of the Witcherverse, sex and sexuality intertwine seamlessly with the realms of politics and magic. Sex serves as a reflection of the mystical forces that mold the world, echoing the ongoing conflict surrounding gender norms depicted across various media within the universe. Just as magic requires

SEXUAL AND RELATIONSHIP ORIENTATIONS IN THE WITCHER

control and purpose amid its inherent chaos, so too does sexuality. *The Witcher* portrays a spectrum of human sexuality, encompassing a diverse range from heterosexuality to pansexuality. Characters occupying the queer end of this spectrum include Ciri, Phillipa, Jaskier, and Prince Radovid, each contributing to the rich portrayal of sexual diversity within the narrative.

Ciri of Cintra

Ciri's bisexuality is evident in the books through her interest in both men and women, a facet not fully explored in the games, particularly her relationship with Mistle. In the books, Ciri's connection with Mistle, the leader of the Rats gang, is primarily physical and experimental, common among individuals navigating their sexual identity, especially in adolescence.

For Ciri, her involvement with Mistle provides a temporary respite from her trauma, offering her physical satisfaction during a tumultuous time. However, as Ciri gains emotional stability, she realizes she isn't in love with Mistle but still cares for her deeply. Unlike those who only value Ciri for her Elder Blood, Mistle genuinely cares for her as a person and respects her fighting abilities.

Their romantic involvement, albeit brief, holds significant weight in Ciri's journey, marking her most meaningful romantic connection in the books. This relationship's inception is hinted at toward the end of the third season of the Netflix series, offering viewers a glimpse into this pivotal aspect of Ciri's character.

In The *Witcher 3: Wild Hunt*, Ciri explicitly confirms her sexual preference for women. Despite this, she has the option to engage romantically with a man named Skjall in a previous event. Their romance is fleeting, ending tragically with Skjall's death as he seeks redemption and validation. Within the Witcherverse, other notable LGBTQ+ characters include the sorceress Philippa, contributing to the varied representation within the series.

Phillipa Eilhart

Phillipa Eilhart, a sorceress trained in Aretuza alongside Yennefer, holds a significant place in *The Witcher* Netflix series as a queer icon, as highlighted by Lauren Schmidt Hissrich, the executive producer and showrunner. Across various adaptations, Philippa is portrayed as a lesbian or bisexual character, consistent with her depiction in the games and novels. In *The Witcher 2: Assassins of Kings*, players encounter scenes depicting Philippa with her lover, Cynthia, offering a glimpse into her romantic preferences. Additionally, references to her sexuality are made by characters like Skalen Burdon, who humorously mentions "lesbomancy" during the "curing" of Saskia the Dragonslayer. Marti Södergren's comment further reinforces Philippa's inclination toward women, noting her disinterest in men.

In the novels, Sabrina Glevissig alludes to Philippa's sexual orientation change over time, a theme echoed in *The Lady of the Lake*, where Philippa wears a sardonyx cameo brooch gifted by her girlfriend, as mentioned by Fringilla Vigo. Even in *The Witcher 3: Wild Hunt*, Sigismund Dijkstra's failed attempt to woo Philippa underscores her preference for women, as revealed in the quest "Now or Never." Additionally, Yarpen Zigrin's mention of Philippa and Dijkstra's involvement, despite her known lack of interest in men, sheds light on her complex relationships and strategic maneuvering.

The novels further delve into the dynamics between Philippa and Dijkstra, emphasizing their connection beyond mere political alliances. The third season of the Netflix series also explores this affair, enriching the portrayal of Philippa's character and relationships within the narrative. Throughout the series, Philippa Eilhart emerges as a multifaceted character, celebrated for her complexity and representation within the LGBTQ+ community.

Jaskier/Dandelion

Jaskier, known as Dandelion in the English versions of the books, presents a distinct portrayal of sexuality across different mediums within the Witcherverse. In the books, Jaskier emerges as one of the Continent's most notorious womanizers, frequently entangled in romantic escapades that often lead to trouble. While his sexual orientation remains ambiguous in the books, his primary relationships are depicted with women.

Similarly, the *Witcher* video games maintain this portrayal of Jaskier as a charismatic ladies' man. In *The Witcher 3: Wild Hunt*, players encounter quests delving into Dandelion's numerous affairs in Novigrad, showcasing his romantic involvement with a fellow artist named Callonetta. Despite leaving ample room for speculation, the games do not explicitly depict Jaskier as bisexual.

However, the Netflix series takes a different approach, hinting at Jaskier's bi- or pansexuality from the first season. Moments such as his immediate fascination with Geralt and suggestive comments, like the one during the viral bathtub scene, suggest a deeper connection beyond friendship. Season 2 further explores Jaskier's feelings in the song "Burn Butcher Burn," where he expresses emotional turmoil regarding his relationship with Geralt. Additionally, in Season 3, Jaskier's partner Vespula mentions his diverse romantic interests, including men, women, dwarves, and elves, indicating his sexual orientation is well-known in the Witcherverse.

Joey Batey, the actor portraying Jaskier, emphasized the care taken to avoid stereotypes in portraying his character's sexuality. This organic development of Jaskier's orientation contributes to the show's inclusivity, aligning with audience demands for better LGBTQ+ representation in media. *The Witcher* series demonstrates an increasing range of relationship orientations, reflecting the complexity and diversity of human experiences within its narrative.

ETHICAL NONMONOGAMY REPRESENTATION

Ethical Nonmonogamy (ENM) serves as an umbrella term encompassing individuals engaged in multiple romantic and sexual relationships, with various labels falling under its scope. Among these labels are swinging, open relationships, relationship anarchy, polyamory, and the "don't ask don't tell" arrangement. Notably, the Witcherverse features several instances of ENM dynamics.

Open Relationship/ENM

In both the video games and the Netflix show, audiences witness Geralt navigating multiple romantic and sexual relationships with various women, although the specific dynamics of these relationships remain somewhat ambiguous due to limited details provided. In the games, Geralt has the option to pursue romantic connections with significant characters like Triss Marigold and Yennefer of Vengerberg, while also engaging in more casual encounters with minor characters such as Keira Metz and Madam Sasha. These situations hint at representations of Ethical Nonmonogamy (ENM), particularly through the lens of open relationships.

Open relationships, a subset of ENM, involve consenting partners engaging in multiple romantic or sexual partnerships simultaneously, without exclusivity. The less committed romantic encounters within the game's storyline seemingly coexist alongside Geralt's long-term goals with Triss and Yennefer, suggesting a level of mutual understanding and consent among all parties involved. This implies that Geralt's relationships with Triss and

Yennefer are likely open, with clear communication and agreement regarding autonomy and boundaries.

Consent is paramount in ENM relationships, ensuring that all partners involved are aware of and agree to the nonmonogamous arrangement. Without mutual consent, engaging in multiple partnerships constitutes a form of nonconsensual, nonmonogamous (NCNM) relationship, commonly referred to as cheating. Assuming that Geralt's romantic partners are aware of each other and have agreed to the terms of their relationships, the possibility for various forms of ENM, such as polyamory, exists within the narrative.

Polyamory

In the Netflix series, there's a subtle nod to polyamory evident in the relationships of characters like Jaskier and Philippa. Those who identify as polyamorous often embrace open relationships and consciously manage feelings of jealousy, rejecting the notion that sexual and relational exclusivity (monogamy) are necessary for deep, committed, and loving connections. In the first episode of Season 1, Jaskier's interaction with his partner Vespula hints at a form of parallel polyamory, where each person maintains separate relationships without intertwining them. Jaskier's relationships also exhibit elements of relationship anarchy, characterized by the absence of predefined structures and hierarchies, allowing connections to develop organically.

Phillipa, Sigismund, and Eva in Season 3 form a "V" or vee relationship dynamic, with Phillipa as the hinge partner. In this arrangement, Phillipa is romantically involved with both Sigismund and Eva, who may or may not be aware of each other's existence. If Phillipa is transparent about her relationships, they might engage in parallel polyamory or hierarchical polyamory, depending on the dynamics and standings within the relationships.

Additionally, Phillipa and Sigismund's interactions provide exposure to power exchange or BDSM relationships within the Netflix series, further illustrating the diverse forms of ENM present in the Witcherverse.

Power Exchange Representation (BDSM)

A component of the BDSM (Bondage, Discipline, Sadism, and Masochism) community, power exchange relationships involve a submissive individual, known as the s-type, granting power and control over aspects of their life to a Dominant partner, referred to as the D-type. Reasons for entering such relationships vary, from spicing up intimate connections to fulfilling a visceral need for control or submission. Crucial to these dynamics are consent, trust, communication, and transparency, often formalized through verbal or written contracts that evolve as the relationship progresses.

In Season 3 of the Netflix series, Philippa Eilhart and Sigismund Dijkstra engage in a Dominant and submissive (D/s) relationship, exploring themes of power exchange. While the books allude to their relationship without delving into its parameters, the show depicts scenes where Philippa assumes a Dominant role, wielding a whip over Sigismund. This BDSM scene represents a consensual play session where participants express creative roles akin to a theatrical performance. In this dynamic, Philippa asserts dominance while Sigismund submits, with these roles possibly influenced by their personalities and heightened during the scene.

Despite Sigismund's authoritative position as the head of Redanian Intelligence and his imposing stature, his desire to surrender control to Philippa illustrates the complexity of power dynamics in their relationship. Philippa, a powerful sorceress and influential political figure, exerts both physical and psychological

SEXUAL AND RELATIONSHIP ORIENTATIONS IN THE WITCHER

dominance over Sigismund, reflecting her formidable influence within Redania's political sphere.

Sigismund's apparent masochistic tendencies add depth to their dynamic but serve to highlight the overarching power balance rather than individual kinks. This scene offers insight into Philippa's commanding presence and strategic prowess, showcasing her ability to navigate both magical and political realms with equal mastery.

In this context, Philippa's Dominance extends beyond her personal relationship with Dijkstra to symbolize her adept navigation of Redania's intricate political landscape. Philippa Eilhart doesn't just wield power; she embodies it, using it as a tool for control and influence. Cassie Clare, the actress portraying Philippa, noted in an interview with HeyUGuys that the dynamic with Dijkstra developed over years of collaboration, fostering complexities and trust within their relationship. This deep connection is a common hallmark of power exchange relationships, evolving incrementally over time with deepening trust and communication.

The Connection Between Trust and Communication

The whipping scene in *The Witcher* series offers valuable insight into Dijkstra's character, presenting viewers with various interpretations of his willingness to submit to Philippa's dominance. It could signify a deep trust in Philippa's judgment, an acknowledgment of the delicate balance of power between them, or perhaps even an expression of his personal inclinations. Regardless, it adds layers to his character, moving beyond the image of the scheming spymaster to reveal a more complex and multifaceted individual. Graham McTavish, the actor portraying Sigismund, highlighted the deep level of trust and vulnerability his character shares with Philippa, emphasizing how this dynamic enhances their mutual dependency on each other.

In the intricate dynamics of a D/s relationship, trust and communication are not just complementary elements; they are the very pillars upon which a healthy and fulfilling dynamic is built. Trust serves as the bedrock of the bond between the Dominant and submissive, anchoring their connection in a sense of security and reliability. Meanwhile, communication acts as the vital conduit through which this trust is conveyed, nurtured, and reinforced over time.

In the realm of *The Witcher*, viewers witness a tangible example of this trust in action during the conclave meeting scene involving Philippa and Dijkstra. Beyond the surface of their exchange lies a deep-rooted trust that underpins their interactions, enabling them to engage with each other confidently and with mutual respect.

Conversely, communication within a D/s dynamic revolves around the open and honest expression of thoughts, feelings, needs, and boundaries. Philippa and Dijkstra exemplify this aspect throughout the third season of *The Witcher*, continuously sharing their plans and fears with one another. Such transparency not only fosters a deeper understanding between them but also reinforces the foundation of trust upon which their relationship thrives.

Indeed, in cultivating an environment of trust, particularly within the intricate political schemes of the realm, open and clear communication proves indispensable. It is through this transparency that both individuals can navigate the complexities of their dynamic with a sense of safety and assurance, knowing that their voices are heard and their concerns respected.

Conclusion

The Witcherverse invests a commendable amount of energy in the representation of diverse populations, spanning from queer to power exchange identities. This commitment serves as a breath of fresh air within the realm of storytelling, as it depicts individuals authentically without relegating their identities to mere plot devices or justifications. Rather than making representation the central focus of its storylines, the Witcherverse seamlessly integrates these identities into its rich narrative tapestry, affirming the inherent value of each character regardless of their orientation or lifestyle choices.

As we reflect on the current state of representation within the Witcherverse, we cannot help but wonder about the future trajectory of its inclusivity. Will the series continue to push boundaries and normalize LGBTQ+, CNM, and power exchange identities even further? This question lingers as an intriguing prospect, hinting at the potential for even greater strides toward inclusivity and acceptance within the world of entertainment.

In the words of Jaskier, immortalized in one of his ballads dedicated to his queer lover, the inclusion of diverse identities in the Witcherverse is not merely a want, but a fundamental need. This sentiment encapsulates the significance of representation in storytelling, emphasizing its role in reflecting the complexities of human experience and fostering a sense of belonging for all audiences. As the Witcherverse evolves, may it continue to champion diversity and pave the way for a more inclusive and empathetic narrative landscape.

About the Author

WENDI "NICKI" LINE, LMHC, CGT is a licensed mental health clinician and a board certified sex therapist in Florida. She completed her masters degree at Liberty University in Lynchburg, VA. Nicki provides care for clients in private practice using an eclectic style. She works primarily with relationships and families. Her niches include trauma, addiction, relationships, sex, LGBTQ+, consensual non-monogamy, kink, and geek culture. Nicki has provided several professional trainings, including The Supernatural Mental Health series for Geek Therapeutics.

References

Allen, S. (2013). Bondage and discipline, dominance and submission, and sadomasochism (BDSM) at the movies. Cinema, Pain and Pleasure. https://doi.org/10.1057/9781137306692.0006

Clinnick, L. (2015). Playing It Safe: Bisexual Representation in Games. PlayWrite. http://playwrite.com.au/playing-it-safe-bisexual-representation-in-games/

Cole, A. (2018). Categories of representation: Improving the discussion and depiction of diversity. TEXT, 22(Special 53). https://doi.org/10.52086/001c.25531

Gray, M. L. (2009). Out in the country: Youth, media, and queer visibility in rural America. New York University Press.

Hissrich, L. (2019). The Witcher. Retrieved November 11, 2024, from https://www.netflix.com/title/80189685.

Látal, M. (2023). LGBTQ+ representation in video games through the eyes of the Queer Community. Iluminace, 34(3), 139–163. https://doi.org/10.58193/ilu.1742

Mocarski, R., King, R., Butler, S., Holt, N. R., Huit, T. Z., Hope, D. A., Meyer, H. M., & Woodruff, N. (2019). The rise of transgender and gender diverse representation in the media: Impacts on the population. Communication, Culture and Critique, 12(3), 416–433. https://doi.org/10.1093/ccc/tcz031

Newmahr, S. (2017). Playing on the edge sadomasochism, risk, and intimacy. W. Ross MacDonald School Resource Services Library.

Sapkowski, A., & French, D. (2023). Sword of destiny. Gollancz.

Sapkowski, A., & Stok, D. (2017). Blood of elves. Orbit.

Sapkowski, A., & Stok, D. (2023). The last wish. Gollancz.

Opie, D. (2023). The witcher was super gay way before Season 3—digital spy. Digital Spy. https://www.digitalspy.com/tv/ustv/a44412387/the-witcher-jaskier-bisexual-gay-season-3/

Rembiś, J., Scharf, J., Villarrubia, J., Otsmane-Elhaou, H., Carpenter, K., Sapkowski, A., Currit, T., & Sapkowski, A. (2022). The Witcher. Dark Horse Books, a division of Dark Horse Comics LLC.

Simula, B. L. (2019). Pleasure, power, and Pain: A review of the literature on the experiences of BDSM participants. Sociology Compass, 13(3). https://doi.org/10.1111/soc4.12668

Sizemore, K. M., & Olmstead, S. B. (2017). Willingness of emerging adults to engage in consensual non-monogamy: A mixed-methods analysis. Archives of Sexual Behavior, 47(5), 1423–1438. https://doi.org/10.1007/s10508-017-1075-5

11

HOW TO TOSS A COIN TO *THE WITCHER*: REWARD AND PURPOSE WHILE IMPACTING THE WORLD

DANIEL A. KAUFMANN

"When you know about something it stops being a nightmare. When you know how to fight something, it stops being so threatening."

— Uncle Vesemir

The world of *The Witcher*, known as the Continent, is a high-fantasy universe rich with moral nuance and constant consequence. For game players, the regions across this map serve as a playground where players, controlling Geralt of Rivia, navigate each territory in search of goal fulfillment and the rewards needed to begin the next quest. Achieving the highest mainstream success of any game in the series, *The Witcher 3: Wild Hunt* contains over four hundred unique quests players can work on, if they are driven to complete every possible story of this renowned (or notorious) witcher. Deciding these many paths is the player's choice, leading to many iterations of the winding narrative. By the end, Geralt can either be firmly remembered as the White Wolf, or he can be cruel to the point where he earns the disdain of many epithets, such as the "Butcher of Blaviken."

Set amid war and constant political tension, we would think a witcher would mostly be hired to slay mythical beasts, when the reality is that the story of Wild Hunt contains a wide variety of adversaries to battle. By the end, it becomes clear that humans are far more capable of evil than even the most feared beasts. When interacting with the full range of morally ambiguous characters, *The Witcher* allows players to truly "live" in a world as unpredictable as it is alluring. This fictional world mirrors our own, presenting moral dilemmas and choice-driven narratives that challenge our perceptions of reward, purpose, and impact.

From the harsh terrains of the Skellige Isles to the politically charged city of Novigrad, every corner of the Witcherverse pulsates with life, promising adventure, reward, and a unique exploration into the human psyche. To define our goals, we must first identify the path. As we learn following the early training with Geralt's mentor, Vesemir, the fantasy playground of *The Witcher*'s world becomes the setting for a profound role-play through human needs, motivations, inner demons, and the perpetual quest for fulfillment.

THE ROLE OF REWARD IN *THE WITCHER*

In *The Witcher*, the concept of reward is multifaceted and deeply intertwined with the game's gripping narrative and intricate role-playing dynamics. These rewards are not merely stat-driven—they are often emotional or moral achievements the player feels as they build Geralt into their vision of who he is in this story. As Geralt navigates the bizarre social scenarios (disgruntled vampires or possessed baby monsters) and demands from political leaders (Emhyr var Emreis in Vizima or the Baron in Crow's Perch), he is tasked with slaying both literal and metaphorical monsters. Indeed, these rewards often come in the form of improved relationships with key characters, alliances formed, or knowledge gained, thus propelling the storyline and enriching Geralt's character development.

Simultaneously, rewards also result in the leveling-up process to enhance Geralt using ability points. These fall under general, combat, sign, and alchemy abilities. It is up to the player to decide what balance of points will result in Geralt becoming the best version of himself. *The Witcher*'s reward system strikes a delicate balance between the psychological gratification of narrative advancement (using Axii to open up new levels of influence over other characters' thoughts) and the practical satisfaction of gameplay abilities, effectively mirroring the complexities of real-world motivations and consequences.

Witcher Sign		Description	Player Type
Aard	⟁	A telekinetic wave that can throw back, knock down, or stun an opponent. This can also destroy obstacles, such as walls or debris.	Acrobat or Slayer Progress through Victory
Axii	⟁	A charm placed on an opponent. If the charm is successful, the enemy becomes an ally for a short period of time, and may even fight at your side.	Architect or Bard Building the Preferred Story
Yrden	⟁	A magical trap placed on the ground used to wound and immobilize opponents. It can also be used to create an impossible barrier.	Ninja or Gladiator Maximum Skill
Igni	⟁	A burst of flames that wounds opponents. Can be used to set objects ablaze or trigger explosions.	Bounty Hunter or Skirmisher Flashy Combat Techniques
Quen	⟁	A protective shield that absorbs all damage directed at Geralt.	Gardener Survive & Win in Time

Figure 1. Witcher Signs matched with psychological
player types and strategies

The reward system in *The Witcher* does more than contribute to Geralt's character development and the narrative's progression; it taps into fundamental psychological processes of classical and operant conditioning. Using scenarios such as Pavlov's dog, where a conditioned stimulus results in a conditioned response, games in *The Witcher* series use the anticipation of rewards (be it a newly upgraded witcher gear or a crucial ally's loyalty) to increase player engagement over time. Every player's choice then becomes a conditioned stimulus. These make players feel internal stress as they choose their dialogue options (or which opponent to slay in battle next) with utmost care. The conditioned response is the excitement and sense of achievement the player experiences when navigating a quest or obtaining a desired reward.

Other scenarios represent what is called operant conditioning. Players quickly learn that their actions and choices—their "operations" in the game world— can lead to positive or negative consequences, effectively reinforcing or discouraging certain behaviors. When the outcome is enjoyable, this increases the likelihood that the player will repeat the action in the future. If the situation goes incredibly badly for Geralt, the player would be less likely to control him in that way in the future. Consider a few noticeable scenarios throughout *The Witcher 3: Wild Hunt*: a sword fight and running down the street of a densely populated city. If a novice player is hit repeatedly by a certain strike by their opponent, they will likely learn to block, parry, or use their signs to shift the battle in their favor. Alternatively, suppose a player is annoyed by the constant grunts of characters who get shoved out of the way as Geralt runs (or rides by on Roach) to the next objective. In that case, they may decide to be thoughtful and move around the NPCs in consideration of their "feelings." The game uses this carrot-and-stick approach, just as originally described by

B.F. Skinner, to make the Path of the *Witcher* a compelling journey of constant learning and adaptation.

 ## THE WITCHER'S PATH: GERALT AND CIRI

The link between in-game rewards and player motivation is represented in Geralt's influence across the entire map. While some activities offer clear rewards like a new weapon or card for Gwent, others, such as the quest "Blood on the Battlefield," present moral dilemmas with wide-ranging relationship consequences for the version of Geralt the player is creating with their playthrough. The latter form of impact creates the challenge that sets *The Witcher* apart from other fantasy games of its era. Instead of simple quest branches that rely on hack-and-slash mechanics and questing for loot, *The Witcher* forces the player to choose how to act in each situation, often unaware of how each choice will impact the quest hours later in the save file.

Geralt's choices also significantly influence his relationship with Ciri in three main areas: narrative outcomes, emotional connection, and Ciri's ultimate path. First, the narrative outcomes of the game hinge heavily on the player's decisions. For instance, dialogue choices during key moments, such as comforting Ciri after she discovers the Elder Blood family tree, directly influence Ciri's fate and the game's ending. Second, these choices also define the emotional bond between Geralt and Ciri. If Geralt acts as a supportive figure, encouraging her independence and showing trust, their connection strengthens, fostering a heartwarming relationship that transcends the usual NPC–Player character dynamic. Finally, the choices impact Ciri's destiny itself. An overprotective or controlling Geralt may inadvertently push Ciri toward a darker path. At the same time, a supportive Geralt helps her embrace her potential, impacting whether she becomes a witcher, an empress, or meets a tragic fate. The decisions made by the player embody the psychological intricacies of human interactions, mirroring the real-world complexities of parenthood and mentorship. This leaves it up to the player to decide how they intend to interact with this highly important character who holds the ability to determine so much of the future of this fictional world.

 ## FULFILLMENT OF NEEDS IN *THE WITCHER*

The fulfillment of basic human needs is depicted through Geralt's actions and decisions, which the player guides. In Choice Theory, originally developed by Dr. William Glasser, the basic needs are survival, love (and belonging), power, freedom, and fun. As a witcher, Geralt is not only concerned about his survival but also seeks gratification through offering food or drink, the awarding of coin, the chance to restore the self through meditation, or satisfying the urges for lust or companionship via sexual encounters. For all the dialogue about witchers being subhuman, the methods in which Geralt pursues the basic needs through his quest choices humanizes him beyond what most game players expect to experience while playing a video game. Ultimately, it is only through the mastery of his witcher senses, combat prowess, and diplomacy skills that quests can be accomplished, allowing these needs to be fulfilled as a secondary consequence that supports the main plot of the Path.

The game beautifully illustrates this through its reward system, where the player's successful strategies in combat, negotiation, and exploration lead to the fulfillment of the need for achievement. At the same time, Geralt's need for sustenance and rest is also addressed in the game. He drinks potions to enhance his abilities, consumes food and water to regain health, and meditates to restore his energy—all of which can be seen as satisfying his physiological needs. Furthermore, the narrative of *The Witcher* also explores Geralt's social needs—his camaraderie with fellow witchers, his complex relationship with sorceresses, and his paternal bond with Ciri, which give him a sense of belonging. In essence, Geralt's journey is not only about slaying monsters and political intrigue but also about fulfilling basic human needs, mirroring the complexities of real-world existence.

By connecting Geralt to the limitations of a human reality using in-game mechanics, *The Witcher* is able to stimulate a deep self-reflection in the player. By taking a moment before and after game time to think about how Geralt has to manage himself in these threatening situations, players can discover how their perceptions influence the decision-making and emotional responses that carry them through their quests in life. The game's reward system, tailored around basic human needs, caters to multiple player desires such as achievement, autonomy, and competence. Players learn about their reactions to dilemmas that mirror real-world situations by making consequential decisions as Geralt. Players weigh decisions based on in-game rewards, emotional satisfaction, and moral judgment in these moments. The game subtly guides players to understand that every choice, as in life, has pros and cons, allowing them to learn about their ethics and values. Moreover, as they navigate Geralt's relationships, players gain insight into their capacity for empathy and relationship-building. In essence, playing *The Witcher* becomes more than just a gaming experience. Rather, just as witchers are transformed into their abilities, our eyes are opened to the mirror of morality crafted by CD Projekt Red to share this journey of self-discovery and introspection with every player who spends time thinking about how they allowed their mindset to influence the experience of the game.

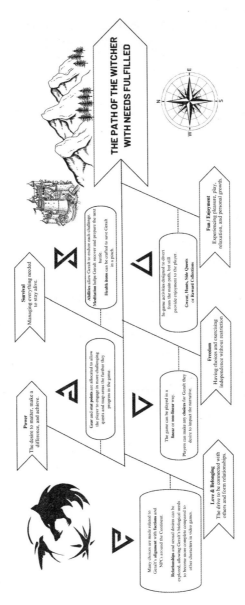

Figure 2. Witcher Signs matched with the Five Basic Needs of Choice Theory

THE MIRROR OF PLAYER MORALITY: NILFGAARD AND REDANIA

The psychological mirror of the *Witcher* series extends to morality as well. In *The Witcher*, morality isn't presented as a binary right or wrong choice. Rather, it unfolds in shades of gray, challenging players to constantly reassess their moral compass. The game's intricate narrative and decision-making system deeply weave in moral considerations, pushing players to reflect on their actions and implications. Players are often faced with complex dilemmas that do not have clear-cut solutions. Hence, the decisions they make are a direct reflection of their personal moral beliefs. This moral complexity is further accentuated by the fact that even well-intentioned decisions can have unforeseen and far-reaching consequences, thus teaching players the intricate nature of ethical decision-making. Therefore, the game does an exceptional job at identity formation; as players navigate through elaborate narratives, engage with various characters, and form relationships, they gain insights into their values, moral beliefs, and ethical standards. Essentially, *The Witcher* does more than tell a story; it provides an introspective mirror, reflecting players' morality and contributing to their identity formation.

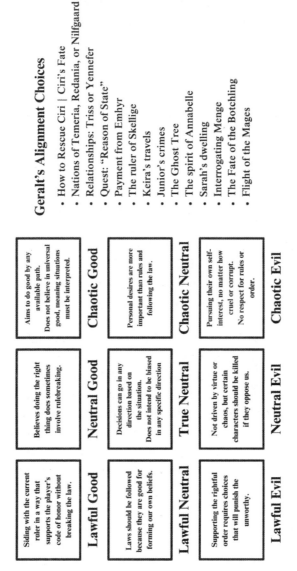

Geralt's Alignment Choices

- How to Rescue Ciri | Ciri's Fate
- Nations of Temeria, Redania, or Nilfgaard
- Relationships: Triss or Yennefer
- Quest: "Reason of State"
- Payment from Emhyr
- The ruler of Skellige
- Keira's travels
- Junior's crimes
- The Ghost Tree
- The spirit of Annabelle
- Sarah's dwelling
- Interrogating Menge
- The Fate of the Botchling
- Flight of the Mages

Lawful Good	Neutral Good	Chaotic Good
Siding with the current ruler in a way that supports the player's code of honor without breaking the law.	Believes doing the right thing that sometimes does involve rulebreaking.	Aims to do good by any available path. Does not believe in universal good, meaning situations must be interpreted.

Lawful Neutral	True Neutral	Chaotic Neutral
Laws should be followed because they are good for forming our own beliefs.	Decisions can go in any direction based on the situation. Does not intend to be biased in any specific direction	Personal desires are more important than rules and following the law.

Lawful Evil	Neutral Evil	Chaotic Evil
Supporting the rightful order requires choices that will punish the unworthy.	Not driven by virtue or chaos, but certain characters should be killed if they oppose us.	Pursuing their own self-interest, no matter how cruel or corrupt. No respect for rules or order.

Figure 3. Dungeons and Dragons Alignment with Choices from *The Witcher 3*

We could argue that siding with the Nilfgaardian Empire in *The Witcher 3* could stem from a player's belief in the concept of utilitarianism—the moral theory that the best action is the one that maximizes overall happiness. Nilfgaard, with its vast resources and structured administration, promises a more orderly and peaceful world once they have conquered the northern kingdoms. Players might sympathize with this viewpoint, seeing the potential for a more stable society united as a single, powerful empire. This perspective aligns with a utilitarian approach, which values the greater good, even if achieving this involves temporary conflict or discomfort. After all, the moral landscape of *The Witcher* is never black and white; it thrives in the gray areas, prompting players to constantly reassess their values and make tough decisions in pursuit of what they perceive as the greatest good for the greatest number.

As an alternative, siding with Redania could be justified by a player's adherence to the ethic of autonomy and self-determination. Redania, despite its flaws, represents an independent northern kingdom's resistance to Nilfgaardian domination. Players who value national freedom may align with Redania, viewing an enforced unification under Nilfgaard as an unjust overreach. This moral standpoint resonates with the philosophical concept of deontology, where decisions are made based on duty, rights, and moral rules rather than their outcomes. In this context, the player might believe it is a moral duty to stand against imperialism, even if the immediate results aren't as comforting as the order promised by Nilfgaard. The struggle of Redania for self-governance could be seen as a morally worthy endeavor despite its leadership's chaotic, imperfect nature. The moral dilemma for this nation relies solely on the player's personal moral beliefs and philosophical leanings.

However, neither Nilfgaard nor Redania in *The Witcher 3* is without their moral shortcomings. Nilfgaard, despite its promise of unity and prosperity, imposes its rule through force and subjugation, often disregarding the cultural identities and historical autonomy of the lands it conquers. Its imperialist tendencies reflect a disregard for the principle of self-determination, creating dissent and resistance among the northern kingdoms. Redania, however, is plagued by prejudice, corruption, and inequity. Its resistance against Nilfgaard often justifies harsh and cruel measures, including ethnocentrism and persecution of nonhumans. Their witch hunts and public burnings for magic-wielders are especially challenging in a world with constant proof that magic is real. The ruling class of Redania is largely indifferent to the plight of the suffering, too distracted by the war against Nilfgaard to attend to the welfare of its citizens.

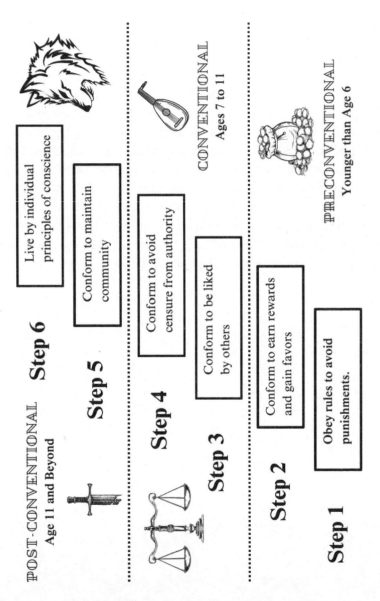

Figure 4. Kohlberg's Stages of Moral Development

With both Nilfgaard and Redania showing moral failings, challenging layers of complexity are added to the player's every political leaning. One of the most powerful differences between playing a video game like *The Witcher 3* versus life in the physical world is that Geralt is empowered to make such a big difference in the world around him. Being morally opposed to something ingrained systemically can allow players to act on their internal reactions to save the world from whichever views they see as a corruption of evil. Rather than being stuck accepting the murder of innocents, Geralt can bring murderers to justice. If something doesn't particularly bother a player, they can choose the true witcher path of neutrality, allowing events to run their natural course. The failings of the Continent reflect the real-world moral landscape, where choices are rarely between absolute good and evil but rather between nuanced and flawed options. By exposing players to these ethical dilemmas, *The Witcher 3* stimulates deeper introspection of our values and the impact of their decisions, further contributing to the game's unique psychological appeal.

PURPOSE AND IMPACT IN *THE WITCHER*

In the *Witcher* games, players are not merely spectators; they are active participants shaping the narrative, their decisions imbued with a profound sense of purpose. This purpose is closely tied to the player's moral and ethical compass and what motivates them to keep playing down the path as Geralt of Rivia. If a player feels strongly about which army should win the war for the North, they can complete the right quests to shift the balance to their favored regime. If they desire a certain set of witcher gear, they can visit the right notice boards to hunt the right monsters to gain the desired attire. Player motivation creates the experience of the game, just as personal motivation determines which life missions a person will be willing to pursue, which calling to answer, and which tasks to complete. When embraced, this active participation and the constant process of gaining experience creates a deep sense of engagement and immersion, providing more than just a gaming experience—it reveals the ideal self, a person the player hopes to become over time. Furthermore, players are given agency to challenge the perceived evils of their virtual world, mirroring real-world morality's complex debates. Such intricate exploration of purpose in a morally complex world defines the unique psychological appeal of the *Witcher* series.

In video games, player agency refers to the player's ability to make choices that actively shape the game's narrative and world or influence the development of their playable character. It is the freedom to make decisions that have real, tangible effects on the storyline, the characters, and the in-game universe. This is not merely about choosing dialogue options or a path to follow; it involves making choices that resonate on a personal level, reflecting the player's values, moral beliefs, and approach to problem-solving. From deciding the fates of kingdoms to choosing who to protect or who to condemn, player agency is at the core of *The Witcher*'s gameplay. It makes players feel their actions matter, deepening their engagement and intensifying their emotional investment in the game. As players move Geralt through the intricacies of a morally complex world, they do so with the awareness that their choices will both reward and punish, creating an echo across the world that defines their unique game experience. This level of agency is a powerful tool for fostering a sense of immersion, purpose, and personal connection with the game, further enhancing its psychological appeal.

The meaningful choices players make in *The Witcher 3* aren't just narrative devices; they give players the agency to shape Geralt's character and the world around him. This can range from influencing political outcomes, deciding who lives or dies, or even shaping Geralt's relationships. When these choices work out as the player intended, it triggers a surge of dopamine in the player's reward system. Often termed the "feel-good hormone," the neurotransmitter dopamine can fire anytime the player makes choices that lead to a satisfactory resolution, such as saving a village from a deadly beast or successfully navigating an intricate political negotiation. The dopamine release reinforces the pleasure derived from decision-making and its ensuing positive outcome, adding an extra layer of immersion to the gameplay. The consequences of these decisions ripple throughout the game, affecting the storyline, characters, and the game world at large. This sense of impact instills a sense of meaning and rewards players with a deeply immersive and personal experience.

Other reward neurotransmitters—such as serotonin, endorphins, and oxytocin—play a vital role in enhancing player engagement and satisfaction. Serotonin, often called the "happiness hormone," may surge when players successfully aid a character they've grown fond of, improving their in-game relationships. This mirrors the real-world function of serotonin in strengthening social bonds and enhancing mood. Similarly, endorphins—our natural painkillers—might be released during intense combat sequences, delivering a sense of euphoria and resilience, especially when the fight's outcome hangs in the balance between success and failure. Finally, oxytocin, the "love hormone," could play a role in crafting deep, emotionally engaging narratives. When players develop attachments to characters or become immersed in romantic storylines, oxytocin levels may change (although likely not as much as nondigital relationships, unless extreme role-play is involved), further allowing for deep engagement with the game's fictional world. As such, *The Witcher 3* is not just a playground for simulated fantasy but also a platform that stimulates our neurochemical reward systems, much like real-world experiences would. Escape, as an element of the immersive experience in gaming, plays a significant role in imbuing the gaming experience with positivity. The game's expansive open world, populated with diverse characters and rich narratives, provides the perfect canvas for players to temporarily leave their real-world frustrations and concerns, seeking refuge in a world bounded only by the limits of their imagination. This detachment from reality offers psychological relief and satisfaction, allowing players to live vicariously through Geralt, becoming a surrogate of the game's protagonist. However winding the path is from the first meeting with Vesemir to the eventual return to White Orchard, immersion creates a deeper connection to the game, increasing satisfaction and fulfillment that enriches the overall gaming experience. In essence, the escape afforded by *The Witcher 3* does more than entertain; it provides a rewarding sanctuary, a place for personal exploration and growth, further enhancing the game's appeal.

The escape motivation allows the game to become a relief from the pressures of daily life. This does not mean that lessons cannot be received during the experience of these much-needed activities. Historically, play has been seen as an important part of human development. As such, gaming (as a technology-based form of play) creates opportunities for new perspectives to form for the person. These ideas help with navigating the complexities of life in any context (including the full experience of our life areas), effectively lowering our risk and encouraging experimentation with our surroundings. Lessons from *The Witcher 3* extend beyond the game's universe, influencing real-life scenarios by promoting decision-making skills, moral reasoning, and empathy. Players sharpen their decision-making abilities by navigating Geralt's world, grappling with ethical dilemmas, and experiencing the consequences of their actions. This provides invaluable practice for real-world situations requiring critical thinking and judgment. Every decision in the game becomes a rehearsal for real-life decision-making, subtly grooming players for better autonomy in their everyday lives.

The improvements in player psychology become the ultimate boon for the gamer, providing a safe space to explore and understand themselves better. The choices players make within the game highlight their personal beliefs, moral principles, and biases, providing powerful insight into their psyche. This self-awareness can foster personal growth and emotional maturity, enhancing interpersonal relationships and well-being. Furthermore, the game's use of reward and need-fulfillment mechanics, such as the satisfaction derived from making impactful decisions or achieving game objectives, can contribute to players' overall mental health by promoting feelings of achievement and competence. This intersection of gaming and psychology enhances the immersive gaming experience and the players' real-life skills and self-understanding.

THE WITCHER'S PATH: YENNEFER AND TRISS

In essence, each choice reflects the player's identity, bringing a level of personal investment and emotional attachment that transcends the virtual realm of the game. Depending on which choice is being analyzed, *The Witcher 3* could be used as an impromptu therapeutic tool, like a personality test, when discussed in a clinical setting. Did the player embark on a relationship with Triss or Yennefer? More importantly, why? This unique blend of player agency and meaningful decision-making sets *The Witcher 3* apart, providing not just a gaming experience but a journey of self-discovery and introspection.

When players choose the path of the enigmatic sorceress Yennefer for Geralt, they embrace a relationship filled with complexity, intensity, and deep-seated love that transcends the ordinary. Yennefer is formidable, possessing an aloof charm and an unyielding will that commands respect and perhaps even intimidation. Opting for Yennefer often signals a player's affinity for profound, layered relationships peppered with a touch of tumult. Additionally, this love is seemingly forced by fate due to a wish made by Geralt in the distant past, before the narrative of *The Witcher 3*. The player is seeking to alter destiny to choose their fate. As a result, this love is as thrilling as it is challenging. This choice may reflect a player's attraction to strength, independence, and a hint of mystery in their real-life relationships. Yet, it's not just about the romantic thrill; it's also about the desire for growth and transformation that such profound relationships often bring, mirroring the player's readiness to navigate the challenges of deep emotional connection, both in the game and beyond.

On the other hand, aligning Geralt's path with Triss Merigold, the fiery yet compassionate sorceress, might indicate a penchant for warmth, comfort, and a sense of familiarity in relationships. Triss's relationship with Geralt is characterized by youthful passion, old friendship, and camaraderie, offering a less tumultuous yet equally fulfilling emotional connection. In the narrative arc of *The Witcher 3*, Geralt has already fallen in love with Triss, but only because his memory has been lost during a near-death experience before the narrative begins. Guided by their shared history and Triss's nurturing nature, players could weave a bond of love and trust that feels less like destiny and more like a choice. Players choosing Triss might resonate with the idea of love that feels safe yet exciting, grounded yet passionate. It could also point toward their preference for an emotional connection that nurtures, comforts, and supports, reflecting their real-world relationship ideals. Therefore, this choice enables the player to shape Geralt's romantic journey and offers subtle insights into their personal relationship preferences and emotional inclinations.

The characters' journey in *The Witcher 3* is intricately woven with the mechanics of reward and need-fulfillment, creating a rich and dynamic narrative experience. Choosing between Yennefer and Triss ripples across the dialogue of the entire game, making each altered scenario obvious yet subtly nuanced. Selecting Yennefer can fulfill a deeper, complex emotional need, with the reward being an intense, transformative relationship underpinned by a sense of epic destiny. Choosing Triss, on the other hand, caters to the need for stability, comfort, and familiar warmth, rewarding the player with a more serene yet passionate romance. Ultimately, this comes down to player preference (or curiosity). Regardless, the narrative adapts to the player's choices, creating a personalized story arc that resonates powerfully with the player's psychological needs and preferences. The game's reward system is not just about external achievements but also about fulfilling internal emotional needs and providing insights into the player's emotional landscape. This blend of narrative control and psychological exploration sets *The Witcher 3* apart, creating a gaming experience that is truly rewarding and deeply fulfilling.

However, *The Witcher 3* cleverly incorporates a cautionary lesson in excessive greed and the desire to have it all. Attempting to pursue a threesome with Yennefer and Triss, driven by the misguided belief that the player can have both these dynamic women simultaneously, leads to an unfortunate and humorous outcome. In a twist of events orchestrated by the two sorceresses, Geralt is left alone, handcuffed to a bed, while Triss and Yennefer share a toast to their successful mischief. This outcome serves as a reminder that greed often leads to empty hands, or in this case, an empty bed. It's an illustrative lesson in the consequences of recklessly trying to fulfill all desires. It reinforces the game's central theme of consequential choices and the reality that every decision —even in love—has rewards and repercussions.

Despite the endless debate around these choices, no matter what relationship is pursued, Geralt always hates teleporting. With complicated real-world relationships, this may be the best takeaway for every player. For a relationship to work, you must be agreeable, but you do not have to enjoy everyone's favorite mode of transportation.

FROM PLAYING GAMES TO BECOMING *THE WITCHER*

In the *Witcher* series, psychological pathways intelligently offer players a unique and deeply personal gaming experience. Through the intricate narrative and consequential decision-making, players find themselves at the helm of Geralt's journey. The game uses the mechanics of reward and need-fulfillment to drive player choices and the narrative. The repeated choices between contrasting desires force the player to build a personal connection with their preferences as they propel the story forward. The game takes this opportunity to cleverly incorporate lessons on the consequences of greed and overindulgence—a pivotal reminder of real-world repercussions for hasty decisions. In these ways, *The Witcher 3* stands out for its ability to create a gaming experience that intertwines personal revelation with a dynamic psychology in its narrative.

About the Author

DR. DANIEL KAUFMANN is an Associate Professor at Grand Canyon University and has served in multiple roles related to program development for gaming and geek therapy training for a variety of clinical settings. His research on the psychology of player types has been presented internationally and continues to evolve with each new world players can inhabit across PCs and consoles. Dr. Kaufmann's publications cover the areas of video games, personality theory, online education, and counselor development. He offers supervision to an international list of clinicians to help bridge the gap in learning about technological impact on society and specific insights related to effectively using games as a positive addition to treatment for clients looking to their gaming activities for inspiration. Dr. Kaufmann is a fearless advocate for the positive elements of video games, and credits them with many of the thought processes that have proved critical in helping him overcome professional and personal journeys in life. As a result, Dr. Kaufmann became more involved in the Geek Therapeutics community in 2020 as a pre senter for online training, content writer, and author. This directly led to using his passion for psychology and mythology to lead him to writing this book, The Gamer's Journey.

References

Bostan, B., & Tingöy, Ö. (2016). Game Design and Gamer Psychology.

Carras, M.C., Kowert, R., & Quandt, T. (2018). Psychosocial Effects of Gaming. *The Oxford Handbook of Cyberpsychology.*

CD Projekt Red (2015). The Witcher 3: Wild Hunt [Video Game].

Klecka, H., Johnston, I.A., Bowman, N.D., & Green, C.S. (2021). Researchers' commercial video game knowledge is associated with differences in beliefs about the impact of gaming on human behavior. *Entertain. Comput., 38,* 100406.

Søraker, J.H. (2016). Gaming the gamer?—The ethics of exploiting psychological research in video games. *J. Inf. Commun. Ethics Soc., 14,* 106–123.

Timofeev, S.B. (2021). Forecasting and Testing the Transformation Potential of Video games. *The Bulletin of Irkutsk State University. Series Psychology.*

Vickery, N.E., & Wyeth, P. (2022). Exploration in Open-World Video games: Environment, Items, Locations, Quests, and Combat in The Witcher 3. *Proceedings of the 34th Australian Conference on Human-Computer Interaction.*

Washburn, D.A. (2003). The games psychologists play (and the data they provide). *Behavior Research Methods, Instruments, & Computers, 35,* 185–193.

Zulkifly, A. (2019). Personality assessment through the use of video games.

READY TO JOURNEY INTO THE

Checkpoints & Autosaves
By the time you reach the last page, you will have a guide to finding common ground with your child that will help you as a parent foster a better relationship, and maybe a new favorite hobby.

Final Fantasy
The Psychology of Final Fantasy guides gamers on a real-world quest of self-discovery so that they can surpass their own limit break.

Dungeons & Dragons
The Psychology of Dungeons & Dragons, is relevant to players, game masters, and even game designers. It applies decades of established and cutting-edge research to help readers understand how playing the game drives behaviors, shapes play, impacts relationships, and changes players once they put away the dice.

Bluey
Through expert commentary, character studies, and thematic explorations, "The Psychology of Bluey" reveals how the show's nuanced portrayal of everyday life can teach us about patience, understanding, and the joy found in life's simplest moments.

My Hero Academia
The Psychology of My Hero Academia" offers a distinctive and contemplative exploration, catering to devoted fans of the series and those intrigued by the psychological impact of storytelling.

Geek Therapy Card Deck
The Geek Therapy Card Deck helps people find balance, reduce stress, bring awareness into their lives, and be mindful in the moment allowing them to manage distress, regulate their emotions and understand life relationships using Geek Cultural Artifacts and insights found within.

GEEK PSYCHOLOGY SERIES?

Meme Life
This book seeks to explain how memes influence societies and cultures.

Pokémon
The Psychology of Pokémon guides gamers on a real-world quest of self-discovery to unravel the mysteries of the Pokémon series.

Elden Ring
Few games have loomed as large in popular video game culture in recent years as Elden Ring, a devastatingly difficult sword-and-sorcery RPG that became a bestseller when it launched on PC, PlayStation, and Xbox consoles back in February 2022.

Gamers Journey
In video games, we are asked to travel through breathtaking virtual creations, all the while collecting a limitless experience which we are fortunate enough to see, hear, and move through as we feel the unleashed joy of our play. This book will bring you through that journey yourself.

The Witcher
Uncover the secrets behind the complex motivations and behaviors of Geralt of Rivia, Yennefer of Vengerberg, and other iconic characters in this captivating exploration of the acclaimed fantasy series.

The Last of Us
In "The Psychology of The Last of Us," delve deep into the hauntingly profound narrative and characters of the groundbreaking video game that captured the hearts and minds of players worldwide.

Visit our website for the full collection of Geek Psychology Series: **shop.geektherapeutics.com**